INVESTMENT APPRAISAL

Investment Appraisal

A Managerial Approach

RICHARD PETTINGER

First published 2000 by
MACMILLAN PRESS LTD
Houndmills, Basingstoke, Hampshire RG21 6XS
and London
Companies and representatives
throughout the world

ISBN 0–333–80058–3 hardcover
ISBN 0–333–80059–1 paperback

A catalogue record for this book is available from the British Library.

This book is printed on paper suitable for recycling and made from fully managed and sustained forest sources.

10   9   8   7   6   5   4   3   2   1
09   08   07   06   05   04   03   02   01   00

Copy-edited and typeset by Povey–Edmondson
Tavistock and Rochdale, England

Printed and bound in Great Britain by
Creative Print & Design (Wales)
Ebbw Vale

 Published in the United States of America by
ST. MARTIN'S PRESS, INC.,
Scholarly and Reference Division
175 Fifth Avenue, New York, N.Y. 10010

ISBN 0–312–23390–6

Contents

List of Figures and Boxes

FIGURES

BOXES

Preface

When making its offerings to prospective clients, the financial services industry is required to declare the following:

'The value of investments can go down as well as up.'

This is clearly understood therefore by all those who buy products – make investments – with the financial services industry.

However, the point is clearly not well understood elsewhere. Research carried out by the Institute of Management in 1997 and the Industrial Society in 1998 found that 87 per cent of all investment ventures either failed or fell short of full success. In addition, they found that corporate investments were either driven by the short-term shareholder value accrued as the result of commitment to investment (rather than completion of investment); or were driven by political factors, prestige, or the dominance of one party in the venture.

Clearly, therefore, there are serious problems to be addressed. This can only take place, however, if a full understanding of the total environment in which investments and ventures take place can be achieved, as well as paying attention to the outputs and financial returns required. Indeed, an accurate understanding of the financial returns that are available can only be considered if the full environment is assessed.

That is the purpose of this book. The view is taken that ventures can only be successful if attention is given to the *full* range of factors present in any situation in which ventures are proposed or contemplated. Chapter 1 is therefore a summary of the structure of the environment in which the ventures take place, and introduces the main principles that have to be considered and applied. Chapter 2 considers the economic aspects and the models normally used to project, forecast and then measure the returns on particular investments. Chapter 3 considers investment strategy and policy aims and objectives.

The remainder of the book is concerned with developing the broader areas that require consideration, and that are all too often neglected. Thus Chapter 4 and Chapter 5 are concerned with the behavioural aspects of investment and decision-making processes. Chapter 6 considers a much broader and deeper approach to the measurement of investment than the familiar practice of concentrating on annual percentage returns. Chapter 7 deals in detail with risk; while Chapter 8 and Chapter 9 consider the problems of establishing and managing effective relations, and the organisational aspects of seeing ventures through to completion. Chapter 10 looks at examples of ventures and investments in practice; and also considers some current initiatives.

The text is illustrated throughout with examples drawn from all areas of activity where investment takes place. This includes: personal finances; the financial services industry; major capital investment; banking, travel, leisure and other commercial services; and the public sector, including extensive references to privatisation ventures and private finance initiatives. The standpoint adopted is that there are lessons to be learned from each of these areas. By identifying and applying a universal set of principles, specific criteria can be established at the outset of ventures to ensure that: all those involved understand as fully as possible what they are seeking or preparing to enter into; the risks involved; and the potential returns available. This is only possible if the broadest perspective is adopted.

RICHARD PETTINGER

SOME INITIAL THOUGHTS

'The predictions of the world's economic forecasters are confounded on a regular basis.'

(Anatole Kaletsky, 'Better than Expected Performance is No Surprise' – *The Times*, 27 April 1999).

Spot the difference:

(a) 'Economists may sometimes seem about as useful as a chocolate teapot but, as this year's Nobel prize for economics shows, it isn't always so. On October the 14th, the $1 million Nobel prize for economics was awarded to two Americans, Robert Merton of Harvard University and Myron Scholes of Stamford University. Their prize-winning work involved precisely the sort of mind-boggling mathematical formulae that usually cause non-economists either to snooze or scream. That is too bad for it ranks among the most useful work that economics has produced. Their work on how to price financial options turned risk management from a guessing game into a science.'

The Economist, 17 October 1997.

(b) 'Like the Titanic, long-term capital management was supposed to be unsinkable. The hedge fund's dramatic downfall and bail out last week was the stuff of Hollywood disaster movies: fortunes laid waste, proud men (Nobel laureates no less) cut down to size, giant tidal-waves threatening to drown some of Wall Street's snootiest institutions at the very least, Wall Street's finest were blinded by the reputations of the LCTM's founders who included Robert Merton and Myron Scholes who last year shared the Nobel prize for economics for their contributions to the understanding of financial risk.'

The Economist, 3 October 1998.

The Yukka Plant

'Ola Pehrsson, a Swedish sculptor, has connected a Yukka plant to a series of electrodes. These are connected to a computer which is, in turn, connected to the share movements on the Swedish stock market. Through its responses to the electrodes and movements on the stock market, the Yukka plant tells Ola Pehrsson whether to buy or sell items in his share portfolio. The experiment commenced in January 1999. By the end of December 1999, the Yukka plant was outperforming analysts working full-time on the Swedish stock market by 30 per cent.'

Ola Pehrsson, interviewed on CNN, 29 September 1999.

'It is apparent that a considerable though closing gap between theory and practice in investment appraisal does exist. It is not credible to explain this away by saying that industry is run by managers who are obtuse and benighted. Neither is it the case that academics are aloof inhabitants of ivory towers churning out abstruse theory. Rather, it should be explained in terms of an in-built resistance to change; of managers favouring the practical and maintaining a healthy scepticism towards theory until it can be shown to work for them. Over time, however, methods of investment appraisal are changing and practice is falling more into line with theory, though how far and how quickly is still unclear. What does seem clear is that there is still room for a more theoretical approach to investment appraisal within commerce and industry.'

R. Dixon, *Investment Appraisal: A Guide for Managers*, Kogan Page, 1994.

'Everything that you do should be directed towards, and directly concerned with, making, selling, billing and collecting. Anything that does not contribute towards one of these elements should be removed.'

Ricardo Semler, *Maverick*, Free Press, 1992.

1 Investment Appraisal in its Environment

INTRODUCTION

The purpose of this chapter is to introduce the context in which investment takes place, and to make it absolutely clear that there is no such thing as a guaranteed return on investment – either in straight financial terms, or anything else that any of the parties involved might have envisaged.

Investment is anything on which a return of any sort is anticipated. Thus people invest time, energy, resources, and also personal interest and commitment in ventures, as well as money.

Investment takes place at all levels. Individuals invest in their careers, development and progress, as well as their prosperity; and there are trade-offs between each. For example, some individuals may forgo perceived quality of life in pursuit of high earnings, and concentrate all their energies on this. Conversely, others take jobs or pursue interests that pay less well financially, but enable them to live in the place of their choice, and to pursue other matters important to them. In the UK, individuals purchase property in the anticipation that there will be a financial return on this; in other parts of the world, this is not so.

Similarly, organisations and the finance industry invest in ventures on which they anticipate returns. In the same way, the nature of the returns anticipated varies between organisations. At the core is a financial drive; however, organisations also invest in reputation, market share, market dominance, prestige and invention, and on each of these activities, returns are likely to be less quantifiable and less certain than, for example, investing in short-term deposits on which there is a guaranteed rate of interest paid.

Governments and other large national and international public bodies (e.g. North Atlantic Treaty Organisation (NATO), United Nations (UN), European Union (EU)) invest for their own reasons also. To do this, they have to raise finance and other resources from those other organisations able to provide them. They then use these to pursue their own priorities; and these priorities arise from political drives and ventures, manifesto commitments, and also matters of political expediency – the need for triumphs, the need to be seen to have achieved something (whether or not the reality is of achievement).

Not-for-profit organisations invest in the welfare and increased quality of life of the client groups that they seek to serve. To do this, they invest in raising money both from the public and also from organisations, which they then direct towards the needs of the particular group of clients.

At this stage it is also useful to define the following:

- *Pre-investment*: the commitment of resources that becomes necessary as a result of initial interest in a venture or proposal. These resources are used to gather information, test for feasibility, conduct market and operational research, and sometimes produce pilot schemes or prototypes before a full commitment to investment is made. At a personal level, once an individual finds or decides that they have resources to invest, pre-investment takes the form of shopping around for the best place in which to commit these resources, having in mind the returns desired.
- *Derived investment*: the commitment of resources that becomes necessary as a result of a particular venture requiring further invention, resources or technology in order that it may be successfully completed. This is a key commitment in pursuit of major public and commercial projects.
- *Parties and partners*: these are anyone involved in a particular project or venture. For ease of discussion, these are defined as follows:

  - investors: anyone putting resources or expertise into a particular venture; this includes shareholders and their representatives, and other backers;
  - venturers: those requiring the investment in order to realise the particular project or venture.

In practice, the distinction is often blurred, because, especially in well-planned ventures, there is, to a great extent, a unity of purpose and direction.

Two useful points may therefore be made initially:

1. Investment is driven by individuals and organisations for their own stated purposes, and the process is therefore at least partly subjective in all cases; this, in turn, means that returns on investment are also calculated subjectively to a greater or lesser extent.
2. What constitutes investment is, to a great extent, a matter of perception, and therefore any scientific approach is limited by the human factors (whether corporate, professional or personal) that are present in every situation.

ORGANISATIONS IN THEIR ENVIRONMENT

All organisations have to operate within the constraints of their environment. All investment therefore takes place in that context. This may be summarised as:

- the internal environment, referring to the organisation's own assets, property, staff qualities, expertise and technology, as well as its financial base, and the ways in which it chooses to combine these for its own purposes;
- the local environment, referring to the place or places in which it operates;
- the competitive environment and markets, referring to the manner in which it sustains and develops its competitive position, serves existing customers and clients, maintains its current base of activities, and wins new business;
- the global environment, referring to the fact that the organisation has at least to be aware of potential for opportunities, threats and competition from all possible quarters.

It is useful to look more closely at the following forces and pressures that the environment constantly brings to bear.

- *Social*: the customs and priorities of the society or societies in which the organisation operates; the wider social respect and regard in which the organisation is held; social perceptions at particular investment ventures.
- *Political*: in which the organisation is under pressure from political drives; and also shapes its investment policies according to political drives (e.g. concern for the environment at the turn of the twenty-first century).
- *Economic*: the availability of financial resources; the propensity to use these resources in particular ventures; the order of priority in which financial resources are apportioned; external financial pressures such as inflation, interest rates and currency exchange rates.
- *Technological*: the opportunities that accrue from technological invention and development; the availability of technology; the availability of expertise to use and exploit the technology.
- *Legal*: the limitations placed on ventures by law; the variation of legal pressures within communities and in different parts of the world.
- *Ethical*: the pressures brought about by what societies, and groups within those societies, consider to be right and wrong; the prevalence and dominance of religious and sectarian interests; concern for issues that are, by common consent, important – e.g. waste disposal, pollution.
- *Competition*: awareness of the actual and potential activities of competitors; pressures brought about as the result of command or scarcity of

resources and expertise; the ability to recoup investment through prices and charges.

- *Market forces*: a nebulous concept concerned with establishing the real and perceived pressures in particular situations.
- *Financial*: a distinction is made between financial and economic forces in the context of investment. This is because in order to stand the greatest possible chance of either making or securing worthwhile investments, it is essential to understand the particular context in which the other parties involved operate (see box 1.1).

Box 1.1   *Investment context: some initial examples*

- *Marks & Spencer*: In the mid-1990s, many firms invested in supplying to Marks & Spencer. They met all quality assurance, deadline, value and delivery dates. The companies came to depend on Marks & Spencer to take enough of their products to secure their own futures. At the turn of the century, Marks & Spencer found themselves in commercial difficulties. This led to radical changes at the top of the company, and a major commercial re-think. Lines of clothing, fresh food and tinned and preserved produce were unilaterally cut. The existing companies found themselves unable to respond to these changes, suffering severe losses or going out of business altogether.
- *National Westminster Bank*: From the 1970s onwards, the National Westminster Bank invested heavily in major overseas ventures. While some of these were successful, producing the desired financial returns, others were not. The company therefore sought to recoup its losses by introducing bank charges to small clients and individual investors. The company was taken over by the Royal Bank of Scotland in February 2000.

In both cases, insufficient attention was given to the context in which each of the parties involved was either forced or required to operate, or in which it chose to do so.

From this, three further points can be made.

1.   There are factors within the control of the parties involved; and there are factors outside the control of the parties involved.
2.   Any investment relationship must have an extent of dominance and dependency.

3.   The likely and possible consequences of ventures must be assessed, as well as the opportunities envisaged.

Once these are assessed and ascertained, it is likely that the desired or required outcomes or returns on investment will have to be at least confirmed as feasible if not modified; and modification may be required upwards as well as downwards. This, in turn, gives rise to the need to consider four interrelated elements:

● the purpose of investment
● the requirement of investment
● the expectations of investment
● return on investment.

Each is now briefly introduced; and each is developed in subsequent chapters.

Purpose of Investment

The purpose of investment is to gain a return, and this is normally assessed in financial terms. However, this needs to be stated as precisely and as realistically as possible.

It also normally requires boundaries of acceptability. This means targeting as precisely as possible; and recognising where if things do not go according to plan, the boundaries – positive and negative – lie (see Figure 1.1).

The purpose also needs a timescale or time frame, both for the whole and also for the steps necessary along the way. This can be dealt with, to an extent, using computer simulations, critical path analyses or performance, evaluation and review techniques. However, it needs broader consideration at the outset because timescales can be changed, extended or contracted as a result of political pressures in public investment; commercial pressures in business investment; or fluctuations in the value of money and interest rates.

As stated above, the purpose of investment is usually measured in financial terms, at least in part. However, other purposes should be introduced at this stage. Investments may be made for any or all of the following reasons.

● *Reputation*: to enhance existing reputation; to gain a broader reputation; to change reputation; to gain reputation in new and unfamiliar areas.
● *Foothold*: to consolidate a foothold in a particular market that now is perceived as being attractive; to gain a foothold in new markets.

(a) Purpose

Financial	*Operational*
● Returns ● Commitment ● Contingencies	● Investment relations ● Dominance and dependency ● Future potential
Social	*Developmental*
● Acceptability ● Concerns, e.g. waste disposal ● Reputation ● Ethical factors	● Future opportunities ● Technology and expertise ● Reputation ● Value

(b)   Boundaries

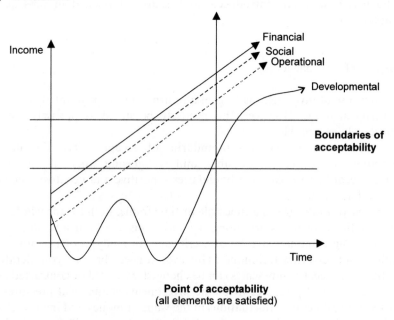

Notes
- The outcomes of all investment decisions should always be assessed and evaluated, and this applies to both success and failure.
- Failure is often easier to assess than success (see Chapter 6).
- Where the upper boundary is greatly exceeded, this is often put down as 'We have succeeded beyond our wildest dreams'. If nothing else, this phrase illustrates just how much investment is, in reality, little more than inspired guesswork or a shot in the dark.

Figure 1.1   The purpose of investment

- *New markets*: to establish a presence in new markets; to find new markets for existing products; to find and develop new products for existing markets; to find and develop new products for new markets.
- *Prestige*: this is where, for example, organisations make investments in building the biggest buildings, tallest towers, the largest ships, the fastest aeroplanes, the most destructive military equipment; and where politicians and others invest in real and perceived triumphs and achievements.
- *Command of resources*: where organisations invest in a scarce or valuable resource, commodity, expertise or technology, either because they need it themselves and it is very expensive; or else to buy up the resource which can then be rationed and sold on to others requiring it.
- *Market expansion and dominance*: in which investment is made either to expand existing markets in volume or returns, or else to drive other players out of a finite market.
- *Desire*: especially the desire to be in a particular sector, market or location. For example, Virgin became an airline because of the desire of Richard Branson to be in the airline industry.
- *Association*: this is often a feature of sponsorship investment or joint ventures. For example, for 20 years Sharp, the Japanese electrical goods manufacturers, invested by association in Manchester United Football Club; ten of the largest construction companies in the UK and France invested in the Channel Tunnel project.

In each of these cases, there is a financial gain expected. However, this will be seen as running parallel to the stated reason; and the returns available are limited by what the investment in these areas can bring with them.

Organisations also invest in their own time, resources, staff, expertise, technology, quality and volume of products and services, markets and marketing in the same ways.

Requirements of Investment

It is essential that these be understood at the outset. For example, if there is a requirement to make a 30 per cent annual return on investment in financial terms, then investment has to be made in sectors where this is feasible. If there is a requirement to complete a particular project in a given time period, then resources must be made available to do this – and this may have consequences for other activities. If investment is required in a particular sector, then it must be acknowledged that the returns on the investment are going to be limited to those that are available in the given sector.

It is further essential that different requirements on the part of all those involved are established at the outset and reconciled. If backers of an enterprise want their money back in twelve months, and the enterprise cannot do this for three years, then the whole relationship needs questioning, because on this basis it is incompatible.

Similarly, if the requirement is not primarily financial, the full situation needs analysis and understanding. For example, if investing in association, the consequences of the failure or loss of reputation of the associate need to be assessed. Or if investing in market dominance, the consequences of substitutes, changes in customer and consumer taste, and responses of competitors, need to be understood (see box 1.2).

Box 1.2   *Requirements of investment: example*

Eurotunnel

In 1986, the Channel Tunnel project was awarded to the proposal made by the Eurotunnel company, a consortium of five UK and five French construction companies. Eurotunnel, in turn, awarded the construction contract to TML, a main contractor also made up of the ten Eurotunnel companies. The stated requirement for investment was in the order of £5 billion over a six-year period. This would consist of money spent on construction costs (60 per cent of the total) and administration and finance charges (40 per cent of the total). The figures were rounded as follows.

	£ million
Building and construction costs	2800
Administration and management charges	700
Provision for inflation	500
Costs of financing the venture	1000
Total capital costs	5000

From this, a number of initial requirements become apparent.

- Sufficient understanding of the construction process and complexities was required to ensure that the project could be completed on time and within provision.
- Sufficient certainty was required in the areas of inflation and finance charges; and it was important that the full boundaries of inflation and finance charges be considered when drawing up the requirements for finance.

- When the project was completed, the operation of the facility must command sufficient price attractiveness, density and frequency of usage to recoup these costs.
- If any of these projections were insufficient, there would be a compounded effect on other resources in the primary pursuit of servicing the finance.

Calculations were then made on the basis of these figures, to arrive at the required frequency and density of usage of the facility. These then became translated into *expected* rather than *required* rates of usage – purely through the human factors present in the enterprise.

The initial lesson therefore is that the required and expected rates of return on any investment must always be kept separate. Once they become interrelated, they gain a life of their own. While not every venture will lose money to the extent of the Eurotunnel project in terms of capital costs and outlay, it is inevitable that confusion will arise if a distinction is not established and maintained.

Expectations in investment appraisal

In practice, expectations that arise as the result of investment initiatives and decisions are almost always subjective and ill-informed; and this is true whether those expectations come from private individuals, managers, financiers, backers or organisations (see box 1.3).

The pressure and limitations of expectations in investment appraisal are developed fully in Chapter 4. At this stage however, it is essential that the influence of expectations on the investment process, and on the overwhelming majority of investments, can be understood.

Return on Investment

At its simplest, this is the return, positive or negative, that accrues to the investor as a result of the investment. For example, an individual investing £1,000 at 3 per cent interest per annum makes £30 as the result of that decision at the end of the year.

Return on investment, however, is rarely that simple. In this case, the 3 per cent is likely either to be set at a sufficiently low level for the financial or other institution to be able to guarantee it, in spite of the factors outside its control; or it will be subject to prescribed rates of interest – which can go up or down, and which are set by governments, national and European Union banks, and are therefore outside the control of those involved. And that is the simple case, involving small sums of money.

Box 1.3 *Investment expectations*

Examples of investment expectations are as follows.

- *Individual*: As stated above, individuals make decisions to buy houses on the basis that they *will* produce a particular positive financial return. They also invest in deposit accounts, personal pensions, school fee plans, on the basis that these *will* produce the projected rate of return.
- *Managers*: Managers take investment decisions on behalf of their organisations, again, in the expectation that they *will* produce the anticipated results. For example, marketing investment *will* produce the projected, desired or anticipated increase in market share, income and profit; recruitment advertising in a particular journal *will* produce a good range (whatever that means) of highly qualified and suitable candidates.
- *Financiers and backers*: Even those providing finance for ventures find themselves anticipating rates of return. This takes the form of: the share price *will* double as the result of involvement in this venture; a particular percentage return *will* be achieved as the result of investment in this venture.
- *Organisations*: Decision-makers in organisations are also subject to the same pressure. This occurs especially where they are being required to act as directed by shareholders and backers' representatives, whether or not they themselves perceive the venture to be in the best interests of the organisation as a whole. The expectational pressures here take the form of for example: 'If we go into this market we *will* make £X million; if we relocate our premises to an area where property is cheaper, we *will* make cost cuts and savings'.

In each case, the quotation at the start of the Preface applies. These examples take no account of anything outside the control of those individuals involved. It is also a useful illustration of how a possible projection can gain a life of its own. As stated above, in practice investment takes place in circumstances in which organisations and individuals have very little overall control.

In more complex cases, the drive is nevertheless to at least pronounce in simple, direct and certain terms. This is superficially attractive all round. In public investments, politicians like to be able to pronounce with certainty on the future outcomes of their actions and ambitions. In commercial situations, this form of pronouncement is what shareholders and other backers wish to hear. However, in practice, if returns are to be predicted with any degree of certainty or accuracy, a great deal more work needs to be carried out.

STAKEHOLDERS

The notion of stakeholders has been popularised in recent years in all walks of life. In the context of investment appraisal, a stakeholder can be defined as anyone who has a particular interest in any aspect of the investment process as follows.

- shareholders, backers, financiers and financial institutions and their representatives
- stock markets, stockbrokers and financial advisers
- organisation directors and shareholders and their representatives
- public service governors and those charged with responsibility for gaining finance and backing for public ventures and enterprises
- organisation directors, managers, staff and their representatives
- commissioners of work
- customers and clients
- industrial and commercial markets
- the communities in which activities are to take place
- the media, business and financial journalists, and media analysts
- suppliers and distributors
- end-users, customers and consumers.
- pressure groups, lobbies and vested interests.

There are therefore divergent interests that have to be considered, and as far as possible reconciled, in any investment proposal.

Dominant Stakeholders

In major investment proposals these are the financial interests – shareholders, backers and other financiers. The response of stock markets also has to be taken into account, as does that of media, business and financial journalists and analysts. Everyone who deals with, and works on behalf of, the finance industry and decides where funds can best be applied in the particular context within which they are requested has to be considered. In some situations, these become over-influential (see box 1.4).

Box 1.4   *Over-influential stakeholders*

In investment appraisal, over-influential players come from two sources.

1. *The finance industry*: If the finance industry is the major source of funds for ventures, it also has its own particular business objectives and targets to meet. Financial analysts and shareholders' representatives may therefore approve or disapprove of a particular venture on the basis of their own narrow interest, in spite of the relative merits or demerits of the particular initiative. For example, a particular merger or takeover may, in the short term, drive up the share price of both (or all) of those parties involved, and therefore become overwhelmingly attractive to the finance industry. The merger therefore goes ahead whether or not it is in the interests of long-term viability and profitability, or whether or not the new merged organisation will be able to deliver products or services as efficiently and as effectively as it did in the past.
2. *Public personalities*: Public personalities affect the success and outcome of ventures because of their sheer force of personality or reputation. For example, building and development proposals envisaged by Norman Foster or Richard Rogers always merit serious consideration because they are dominant public figures in their field, as well as experts. Conversely, the value of the investment in the extension to the Natural History Museum was seriously damaged by comments made by the Prince of Wales that 'It is a monstrous carbuncle on the face of a well loved friend'.

Knowledge and Influence

All parties in investment initiatives bring with them certain amounts of knowledge and influence. This may be plotted on the following spectrum (see Figure 1.2).

It is important to recognise that dominant stakeholders may come to a situation from one extreme. It is especially true that many financiers are asked to put resources into an initiative of which they have little or no personal knowledge. It is also true that many financial journalists and analysts see finance and investment purely from the point of view of the performance of share prices, short-term company profitability and media reputation, without any reference to customer confidence and satisfaction or the residual value of the facility to end-users (see box 1.5).

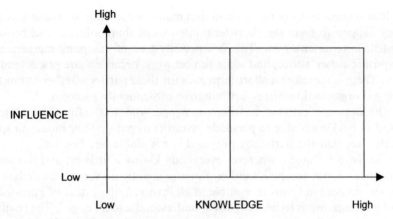

Figure 1.2   *The knowledge–influence spectrum*

Box 1.5   *Electrolux*

Electrolux is a Swedish multinational organisation, and is well known for producing washing machines, tumble dryers, refrigerators, freezers and cookers.

In February 1993 the company announced that it was cutting its dividend. For the previous two years, in spite of downturn in demand for products and falling levels of profit, the company had paid the dividend out of retained profits. This had sustained the share price and attractiveness of shares for the previous two years.

In response, the company shares fell by 6 per cent. This was because of adverse comments by financial analysts and media commentators. Because of the ways in which this move was reported, it also damaged consumer confidence in the company's goods. This was in spite of the fact that the company had increased productivity, product reliability and quality, and had been able to maintain prices in order to retain general market attractiveness. The company had also gained a foot-hold in the giant US white goods market, and had been able to compete on price as well as reliability and after-sales guarantees.

This illustrates the conflicting pools, and the dominance of financial and media analysis over the long-term business drive to produce high quality goods and services required by customers. It also illustrates the damage to companies that can be caused if it is known, believed or perceived not to be performing well from the point of view of one dominant stakeholder.

It also needs to be borne in mind that many investments are made because they happen to be in the short-term interests of shareholders, stockbrokers and their representatives. This is especially true of company mergers and acquisitions (see above) and some project work because share prices tend to rise. There is therefore a short-term gain for these parties whether or not the merged organisation or project initiative subsequently succeeds.

The opposite extreme is where someone who has influence and who requires backing is able to persuade investors to put up their money in spite of the fact that the particular proposal is not viable (see box 1.6).

Clearly, a balance – wherever everybody knows a little bit and has some influence – is not acceptable either. For any investment venture and relationship to succeed in terms acceptable to all involved, the extent of knowledge and influence needs to be recognised, understood and managed. The result is therefore as full a mutual understanding and confidence as possible.

Pre-investment Groundwork

It is essential that pre-investment groundwork is carried out, and a large part of this is with the purpose of gaining satisfactory knowledge on the points so far discussed. It also needs to cover from the point of view of the particular proposal and the context in which it is being made:

- the range of returns possible, both positive and negative, and in financial and non-financial terms
- determination of policy and direction for the particular venture
- attention to the behavioural aspects of the venture
- assessment of the risks involved in the venture
- definitions of success and failure, aims and objectives, in terms acceptable to each party to the venture
- processes for the management of the venture, and the relationships generated as a result
- general levels of acceptability or otherwise of involvement in the initiative
- the priority of the initiative in the portfolio of each of those involved
- the length of time for which investment is required and the extent to which this may contract (and especially) extend; and the acceptability of this to all concerned
- the consequences of success
- the consequences of failure.

Such groundwork enables a much greater understanding of the overall context of proposals for investment, whether in individual initiatives, business ventures or public services. It may also lead to the necessity for schemes and ventures to be piloted or pre-tested to try and gain a better understanding of whether the venture is likely to succeed when it is fully engaged.

Box 1.6 *Viability and personality*

Robert Maxwell

Robert Maxwell came to the UK in 1943 from Czechoslovakia. He was a refugee from the Nazis, and had escaped certain death. He enrolled in the Royal Air Force and became a war hero, winning the Military Cross. He subsequently became a Labour MP, and also founded his own publishing empire.

Because of his achievements, and the sheer force of his personality, he was able to attract investment whether or not the particular ventures proposed merited it. Eventually business focus was lost and he had to resort to stealing from his employees' pension fund in order to sustain his business ventures and publishing empire, including the *Mirror* newspaper. However, he was still able to attract investment funds from sources which continued to have confidence in him even during the weeks before his death (widely believed to have been a suicide which he chose rather than having to face full-scale fraud and mismanagement applications).

Freddie Laker

In 1978 Freddie Laker founded Laker Airways. Laker Airways was different from big national airlines, in that it offered non-bookable and non-refundable transatlantic crossings at extremely low prices. Laker engaged the interests of the media and politicians, and the airline was launched amid a great blaze of positive publicity. Prices charged for an Atlantic crossing were £50 one-way (approximately £80 at Year 2000 prices), and for a considerable period of time the planes flew full each journey.

The company experienced short-term cash flow problems, and also competitive responses from the big airlines that bordered on restraint of trade. A major London clearing bank was persuaded to underwrite the company for a period of three years. At the end of the three-year period, the bank decided to pull out of the venture and have it declared bankrupt. The bank was then persuaded to back Laker for a further three years. Three years later, the bank refused to underwrite Laker Airways any further. It pulled out of the venture with losses of £110 million.

Business Cases for Investment

Business cases are at the greatest risk of dominance by stockbrokers, shareholders and their representatives, who invariably wish for an initiative to go ahead because of the short-term gains that may be made. This especially applies to mergers and takeovers.

Where this is not the case, attention has to be paid to the length, duration, balance and management of the relationship. This was referred to briefly above and needs to be designed and determined at the outset of any venture (see box 1.7).

The whole has then to be capable of detailed scrutiny from the point of view of all stakeholders. In many cases, potential disasters can be avoided if the broader perspective is adopted at this stage, rather than concentrating on the narrow and dominant – and short-term – financial advantages that may accrue to one group.

Finally, reference must be made to the profit motive. Different parties will measure this in different ways; but at the core are some yardsticks common to all situations:

- the extent to which this helps to ensure long-term organisational survival, viability, profitability and value;
- what the commercial relationship with customers, clients and end-users is to be based on;
- whether the venture is sustainable on its own, or whether it needs additional support from the parties involved;
- what else it is likely to lead to.

These are the grounds on which long-term, sustainable, commercial profitability is based in investment ventures.

Public Service Cases for Investment

The public sector makes much of its investment in the form of commissioning and underwriting public works. These are overwhelmingly infrastructure (e.g. roads, railways); information, communications and technology; emergency services including health and defence; core public services such as health, education, policing, environmental and waste management; and public amenities such as sports and leisure centres.

These works are commissioned for a variety of reasons:

- to meet political manifesto commitments
- to provide an acceptable quality of life for the people that they represent
- to provide basic amenities and services

- to maintain, enhance and improve education, health care, social service and infrastructure
- to undertake *pump-priming* activities based on the premise that, if public investment is made in a particular area or activity in the first place, it will draw in further commercial investment
- to respond to community priorities
- to enhance and improve society at large.

In the past, those organisations that invested in public works, or concentrated on winning local and central government contracts, did so because of the certainty of continuity of work. This has all changed to the extent that in the UK at least, it is becoming very difficult to find organisations that are prepared to carry out public projects without guarantees which government bodies are increasingly reluctant to give.

It is certainly true that some initial clarity of understanding is required before any investment is made. This must also include:

- reference to individual and collective political drives, including party political priorities;
- recognition that politicians associate and dissociate themselves with ventures according to political feelings rather than investment integrity (see box 1.8);
- recognition that those governing public ventures may change every four years in local government, and every five in central government; and that this affects the constitution of other public bodies such as the National Health Service, and also privatised industries such as rail, gas, electricity and water;
- recognition that very little of this is inside the control of those who undertake investment ventures on behalf of the public sector.

It is also true that both local and central government impose changes to all aspects of their investment programmes at very short notice. Those to be most aware of at this stage are:

- moratoria or cuts in public spending, leaving the contractors and other investors with cash flow problems;
- changes in policy direction requiring more work for the same money, or else unilaterally cutting the money available to underwrite work in progress;
- changes in political priority and confidence, meaning that work commissioned is effectively no longer required;
- consequences of engaging in this form of investment relationship (see box 1.9);
- the annual public service budgeting and resourcing cycle, by which public budgets are allocated and confirmed every twelve months.

Box 1.7   *Some initial questions for business cases*

Investor:

Are we satisfied with our own level of product/service/market knowledge?
Have we had/do we need any independent appraisal?
What are the consequences of success? What are the consequences of failure?
What changes in market conditions, technology, fashion and durability may be envisaged?
What changes in policies, direction and priorities may be envisaged?
What is the return on investment that we wish to make? That we need to make?
What are the levels of profit that we wish to make? That we need to make?
Have we confidence in the professional capabilities of those also involved in delivering our requirements?

Other Venturers and Stakeholders:

Why are we using these backers? Is it because we have to? Because we want to?
Are they the best for our venture? What does 'best' actually mean?
What is our experience of using these backers in the past? What is other people's experience of using these backers in the past?
Are we satisfied with the terms and conditions of involvement of the investors?
What are the alternatives to using this particular approach? Is this the best way forward? Again, what does 'best' mean?
What are our desired and required returns on investment? What levels of profit do we seek to achieve?

Both:

Who has control? What does the extent of this control (or lack of control) actually mean? What are the consequences and implications? Are there are any questions of veto? What is the basis on which the project will either go ahead or be cancelled? Is this acceptable?

In many cases, these questions are either not addressed at all, or else only partially addressed. The personal and professional drive to get a venture off the ground tends to lead to a process of editing out all of those areas that are more difficult to address or manage.

Box 1.8 *The Millennium Dome*

The Millennium Dome is being built on the south bank of the River Thames near its estuary at Greenwich. It was commissioned at a press conference in 1992 by the then Conservative Government. It was then confirmed as going ahead in 1994 also at a press conference. It would become, so the press release stated, a focal point for the celebrations of 2000 years of Christianity. Everybody would want to visit it. It would have a variety of exhibitions representing all aspects of life of the previous thousand years; while at its core would be a Christian and spiritual theme reflecting the fact that the 2000 years that it was celebrating had been counted from the date of the birth of Jesus Christ.

The project was confirmed as going ahead in June 1997 following a change of government. However, because the project was required to be completed by 31 December 1999, the government had to put serious effort into raising sufficient finance and interest to ensure that it could be built. Consequently, the project was scaled down; and such sponsorship as was attracted was only achieved because of substantial political arm-twisting. There was also to be no central Christian theme, because backing could not be found from Christian churches; Hinduism provided the main religious interest.

The Government sought to rescue the project by promising that the site would be redeveloped to provide better facilities and a national monument for all. Those who have invested in the project have been promised that they can sell the site on as soon as this becomes profitable. Several organisations – notably the Disney Corporation – have declared an initial interest.

However, in order to gain a financial return on investment, the Dome was dependent on an average visitor flow of 12,000 per day. The venture ran into difficulty when it became clear that this was not possible. This was compounded by adverse media coverage, and transport and access problems. The top management team was replaced and reconstituted in February 2000.

CONCLUSIONS

As stated at the outset, it is necessary to understand the broad context in which investment takes place and to understand how this both helps to shape and also to limit the scope for effective ventures.

Box 1.9 *Public sector investment in the construction industry*

Over the period 1945–75, the construction and civil engineering industries in the UK depended on government for large volumes of work. Many companies in these sectors came to depend on it. A productive and positive – if often expensive – mutual relationship was enjoyed over the period.

This relationship was disrupted when recession and inflation required cuts in government expenditure. As a result, large companies in the industry cut jobs. Many smaller companies, especially subcontractors and specialists went out of business and the industry altogether.

Subsequently, government attempted to revive the relationship. However, they based it on a combination of competitive tendering, cuts in investment levels and therefore profit margins, and requirements to bid for large tranches of work over long periods of time. The results were as follows.

- Many domestic companies were no longer big enough to carry out the work required because they had cut back so sharply.
- Companies that were large enough to bid for, and carry out the work, often came from overseas, therefore exacerbating the balance of payments problems on which the government bases its financial decisions and projections. The problem was exacerbated because non-government clients saw the perceived improvement in project deliverability and quality, and therefore they too sought contractors from overseas.
- Companies that were awarded work on the basis of the lowness of their price subsequently found that everything else about the relationship was wrong. This especially referred (and continues to refer) to the fact that governments and public bodies will unilaterally switch contractors if they believe it in their interests to do so.
- The best companies were, in any case, able to secure work away from the government. They were therefore no longer dependent on it.

The consequence is that those seeking to make investment in public service activities, now seek (and often receive) assurances that any changes in political priority or public spending arrangements will be underwritten. This has compounded the problem of there being less work; and such projects as are commissioned are now more expensive and more difficult to deliver.

It should be clear that investment is a process, and that this process is not linear. Investors may not get their desired rate of return on the precise date that was targeted at the outset of the initiative. Or it may be that the level of resources raised was insufficient for the particular initiative. There is no other way to consider this from a business point of view other than to keep it under constant review.

It should also be clear at this stage that investment is not just a financial activity. It involves a variety of behavioural and perceptual business and organisational factors, each of which has to be successfully engaged if effective investments are to be made.

All parties may also engage in investment relationships because they anticipate further work in the sector or with each other. Again, this needs to be understood at the outset. If it is not, one party may be unwilling to continue to support the matters currently in hand.

Guarantees of future work contracts and initiatives also have to be seen in the broadest possible context. All organisations experience staff changes as well as changes in organisational direction. As the result of any or all of these, the particular initiative or partnership may no longer be attractive, or may only continue to be attractive if further changes are made in the business relationship.

Finally, this chapter has sought to introduce the range of factors that need to be taken into account. These are dealt with in the subsequent chapters of the book. At the core of this is finance. It is now necessary to turn to this aspect of investment appraisal.

2 Economic and Financial Information

INTRODUCTION

The purpose of this chapter is to provide a summary of the economic accounting and financial models and conventions that are used to provide the information that forms the basis of evaluating investment proposals, and taking decisions. The approach is designed to ensure that each model is explained in simple and direct terms. It is also essential that the vagaries, uncertainties and shortcomings of each are understood if effective, profitable and sustainable investment decisions are to be taken.

BARRIERS AND ASSUMPTIONS

It is first necessary to recognise the barriers and assumptions that exist wherever economic and financial information is requested. A simple model of this can be seen in Figure 2.1.

Figure 2.1 represents a simple form only; the problem is compounded every time more complex information is required or where it is requested

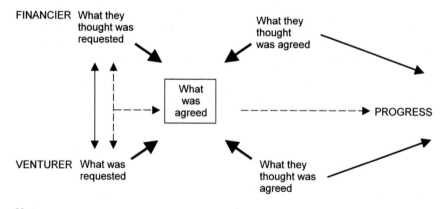

Note:
Each full arrow represents an area where misunderstandings occur; each broken arrow indicates the assumption that the job was perfectly carried out and understood.

Figure 2.1   *The nature of barriers and assumptions*

from a variety of sources. The initial lesson, therefore, is to ensure that full and effective liaison is established between investment information experts and decision-making bodies to ensure that the assumptions and barriers are broken down. This, in turn, leads to a much greater mutual understanding of the real range of pressures and priorities (see box 2.1).

Box 2.1 *'We took the decision based on the best information that we had available'*

This is almost invariably untrue. In practice, there is always sufficient information available to base decisions on the long-term viability of ventures (or not), or to predict with a fair degree of certainty the range of possible outcomes of a particular venture.

The problem lies in the understanding and assessment of the information; and of the other forces present when the decision is taken. In practice, most decision-makers consider the information in the context of satisfying short- to medium-term shareholder or owner interest, or (in the case of public ventures) political drives and initiatives, and budget constraints.

The process is therefore normally tainted by:

- *partiality*: in which one party either wishes the venture to go ahead, or else wishes that the venture does not go ahead, and therefore uses the information in support of this preordained point of view;
- *over-mightiness*: in which the interests of one dominant party become the overriding reason for it to go ahead;
- the interest of *short-term gain*, which is especially fuelled by the fact that any consultants, lawyers or investment analysts see their returns at the inception of the venture and not its completion.

This represents the overall context in which all investment decisions are taken and in which the following approaches are used.

Time

It is usual to distinguish three time frames:

- short-term, which is attractive to all concerned, because the outcome and returns on a particular venture are easier to predict with a greater degree of certainty than when the time period is extended; it is also a favoured

strategy of those concerned with the assessment and management of risk
to reduce, as far as possible, the time frame involved in calculating returns
on investment because, again, acceptable rates of return can be calculated
with a greater degree of certainty;
- medium-term, which normally covers the period of commitment to
  purpose, and initial activities for large ventures; and for fixed-term
  ventures (e.g. when pay-back is desired over periods of 2–5 years);
- long-term, in which elements of risk have to be identified, assessed and
  managed.

Time frames are a feature of particular industrial, commercial and public
sectors, and consequently short-, medium- and long-term have different
connotations according to the sector in which investment is contemplated.

Time is also used as a variable in calculating net present values,
depreciation and net rates of return (see below).

Time is also a key feature of accounting conventions. Companies are
legally obliged to produce annual reports; and these represent a true and fair
reflection of the effectiveness of application of shareholder's funds. Shareholders expect share values and dividends to increase; and consequently, the
value of investments has to be written into the annual report to show the
effectiveness of the decisions made. Problems arise when the annual report,
and reporting relationships between shareholders and decision-makers,
become the driving force for the assessment of investments and other work
in progress.

In the public sector, there are also problems of this nature with annual
budget cycles. Those who invest in public services may therefore find
themselves unable to proceed with the venture as they would prefer; the
archetype of public availability of funds is given below (see Figure 2.2), and
this still remains the norm.

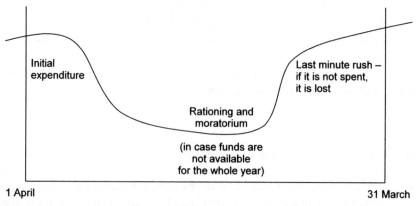

Figure 2.2   *Application of public funds*

Finally, money itself has a time value. A unit of currency is valued more highly than at some time in the future; but lower than at a time in the past. This is largely because inflation is an ever-present factor in modern economies. This erodes the value of money as a means of exchange, and as a *reckoner* of value. Inflation reduces purchasing power and the extent to which a currency is at risk of inflation (i.e. the rate at which it is losing its value) also causes questions of confidence. For example, over the period 1998–99, the Turkish lira lost half its value and similar problems were encountered with currencies in the Far East in the period 1997–98.

The consequence of this is that both individual and corporate investors prefer to have their money now, or failing that, as quickly as possible. Again, this is because the value of the money, and its purchasing power, can be predicted with a greater degree of certainty the sooner it is received.

COSTS

It is usual to distinguish between the following:

- *Fixed costs (FC)*: These are the costs incurred by organisations whether or not any business is conducted. They consist of capital charges, premises costs, staff costs, and administrative, managerial and support function overheads.
- *Variable costs (VC)*: These are the costs incurred as the result of engaging in activities. They consist of raw materials, packaging and distribution costs; and the frequency and density of usage of equipment (e.g. production technology, telephone, and information systems).
- *Marginal costs (MC)*: This is the cost incurred by the production of one extra item of output and reflects the extent to which production capacity may be extended without incurring additional fixed costs in the forms of investment in new plant, staff, equipment and technology.
- *Opportunity costs (OC)*: Opportunity costs represent the opportunities forgone as the result of being involved in one area in preference to others.
- *Total cost (TC)*: Total cost is the summary of all costs incurred by organisations as the result of engaging in particular ventures. It is the summary of fixed costs, variable costs, marginal costs and opportunity costs.

This is overtly straightforward. There are problems, however, as follows.

- It is true that fixed costs can be varied over the medium to long term. Varying fixed costs always incurs short-term charges and additional expenditure, even if the intention, in the long term, is to reduce the fixed cost base. Involvement in new technology or projects always involves an initial outlay; the sale of further shares normally includes discounts to existing shareholders. Redundancies always increase costs because they mean that, in the short-term, people are to be paid additional amounts to leave their job. Sales of assets – residual products, technology, property – normally means that these items have to be written down; there is usually a substantial difference between the value placed on these items, and the real returns that accrue when they are sold.

- Producing additional items out of the existing cost base is extremely attractive; and the greater capability to get as near as possible to 100 per cent productivity or potential, the greater the returns on the capital and assets employed. Problems arise where the '100 per cent' is miscalculated. This means that either output and venture facilities are over-extended causing stresses and strains; or else they break down altogether, which requires investment in either maintenance, refurbishment or replacement.

- There are also problems with the management of opportunity costs. Once it becomes apparent that funds, resources and expertise are available to invest in new ventures, it is possible to become bogged down in extensive consultation and research processes, with the result that any opportunity initially apparent may be lost. It also introduces the point that it is impossible to take perfect decisions. While it is necessary to understand the range of opportunities that are on offer at a particular time, once the decision to go with one of them is taken, this must represent commitment to purpose (see box 2.2).

Box 2.2   *Consideration of costs*

Labour Costs

Many consider labour costs to be variable. This is almost always not true. The nearest to variability that companies and organisations can genuinely get to a variability in labour costs is either to relate performance directly to productivity and effectiveness, for example through the use of performance-related or profit-related pay schemes; or else through putting employment out to tender and subcontract (in which case, there will be a fixed price for the labour once the contract is agreed). Moreover, when variations in the labour force are required through redundancy, retraining, redeployment or redevelopment, there is an immediate additional cost to be borne. Job evaluation also brings additional costs related to the engagement of consultants, the consideration of cases, and the resolution of anomalies. The only variation therefore in the price of labour, in the short to medium term at least, is upwards.

Technology and Equipment Costs

While these may be depreciated over periods of time by accountants quite legitimately through the use of accounting conventions, in practice:

- The purchase of equipment may be required immediately, whether or not the previous technology has been fully written off or depreciated.
- Also the equipment may become obsolete overnight, again whether or not it has been fully written off or depreciated.

There is therefore a clear distinction between the accountancy and managerial approach to investment in technology and this needs always to be maintained.

A Behavioural View of Costs

Observations carried out by McKinsey in the 1980s led the researchers to conclude that whenever a company found itself in short- to medium-term financial difficulties, it would engage in any or all of the following:

- confrontational relationships between itself and any recognised trade unions; cutbacks in training and development activities, especially for those lower down the organisation;
- the removal of tea and coffee making facilities and machines, and the removal of flowers and magazines from the reception area.

Source: T. Peters, *The World Turned Upside Down*, Channel 4 Television, 1986.

The Costs of Capital

Commercial organisations draw their financial resources from:

- the sale of shares either to family, friends and colleagues; or else on stock markets;
- the sale of loan notes and debentures which may be described as short-term or fixed-term capital and which must be repaid on the date specified;
- government grants and incentives issued either in the form of regional aid, start-up and *pump priming* funds, and guarantees; or else in return for undertaking government contracts;

- retained income, surpluses and profits from activities carried out;
- bank and finance house loans on which interest is repayable over the period of the loan;
- share capital has a perceived or indicated cost attached to it in that shareholders expect a dividend commensurate with the levels that they have been led to anticipate; they also expect ventures to be conducted in such a way that the commercial value of the shares will rise;
- loans have contracted charges in the form of interest repayments or – in the case of debentures – a deadline on which the money outstanding has to be repaid;
- retained income surpluses and profits have managerial and expertise charges placed on them to ensure that this part of the resource is used as effectively and profitably as possible so that it becomes less necessary for further share or loan funds to be sought.

Gearing

Gearing is the relationship between bank loans and other sources of finance. The convention in the West is that gearing should be as low as possible, meaning that the balance of financial resources should depend as little as possible on bank loans.

Gearing may be expressed as the following ratio:

$$\text{Gearing} = \frac{\text{Bank loans}}{\text{Share liabilities}}$$

Percentages can then be calculated, and assessed for suitability and viability.

The higher the level of capital gearing, the greater the risk associated with the company. The gearing ratio should always represent a key point of enquiry in the assessment of risk (see Chapter 7).

High levels of gearing may have implications for cash flow, in that interest charges are a contracted cost of capital and have to be paid when required. In long-term capital ventures, this may bring the additional cost of having to provide extensive overdraft facilities.

When high profits are being made, high gearing provides shareholders with high returns on their investment. This is because interest charges are written out of the equation before the profit on which the dividends and returns to be paid are calculated.

Borrowing is also attractive when inflation is high – especially when it is higher than the percentage rate of interest required. If a company borrows money at an interest rate of 5 per cent per annum, and inflation is running at 5 per cent per annum, then the funds are effectively free of charge. If inflation is any higher than this, then it is effectively being subsidised in its venture by the loan maker.

Other costs and charges that have to be written in are:

- liability for taxation over the duration of the venture;
- servicing inflationary pressures, where the value of one of the currencies being used is declining steeply in value;
- and assessing maintenance upgrade and replacement charges for each aspect of the venture.

This involves the creation of capital cycles as follows:

- *Taxation cycles* – taxation volumes, frequencies and regularities of payments demanded by government (or governments if it is a multi-national or international venture). This is also a key issue for those investing in small business ventures in the UK where taxation for the current year is pre-assessed by the Inland Revenue on the basis of the previous year's trading (and any tax credits that subsequently become due are paid a year in arrears by the Inland Revenue).
- *Inflation cycles* – underwriting or insuring against the effects of inflation are extremely difficult to achieve; and this is a further problem when conducting long-term ventures, because long-term inflation rates are extremely difficult to predict; again, therefore, this becomes a key point of enquiry when assessing the risk involved in particular ventures.
- *Replacement cycles* – replacement cycles are concerned with the operational aspects of investment. Referring especially to technology and expertise, replacement cycles have to be calculated in order to obtain the best possible returns on technology before it reaches the end of its useful life; establish pay and reward rates that are likely to attract, retain and provide incentive to those with the expertise required.
- *Crisis replacement cycles* – these must also be built in to this part of the process so that breakdown of equipment, or the sudden loss of key expertise, can be addressed quickly.

ASSETS AND ASSET VALUES

Assets are required by organisations to enable them to pursue their stated purposes.

Capital Assets

Capital assets consist of premises, technology, equipment, machinery and expertise to be used in the production of the required outputs of the venture. They are sometimes referred to as fixed or tangible assets. Their acquisition is based on a combination of what the venture can afford, the projected length of the asset's useful life, and the uses to which they are best suited.

Intangible Assets

Intangible assets consist of reputation, expertise, information, goodwill, confidence and expectation levels. They reflect part of the basis on which those interested become involved in ventures. High levels of goodwill and expectation are normally anticipated to translate into high levels of repeat business, increased reputation, and enlargement of customer demands and customer bases – and therefore profits and effective activity.

Asset Values

Brand names, and the reputation of key figures, are also regarded as assets. Strong brand names (for example, Coca-Cola, Nescafé, Barbie) carry high and continuing levels of value. They each also have commercial values in their own right and could be put up for sale if the owning company so desired.

This also applies to key figures. A key feature of the asset value of the Virgin Group is the presence of Richard Branson; and the same applies to Anita and Gordon Roddick at the Body Shop (see box 2.3).

Box 2.3 *Key personality: asset or liability?*

An alternative view of this is to see the presence of a key personality as both asset and liability.

For example, while a great deal of confidence is invested in the Virgin Group as the result of the presence of Richard Branson, some analysts have voiced their concern over what would happen to the group, were anything to happen to Branson himself. This also applies to the Roddicks at the Body Shop.

Other examples abound. Investors are concerned with what might happen to Manchester United Football Club when Alex Ferguson (the Club's manager from 1986 to date) leaves or retires. This, in turn, gives rise to a more general consideration of the (entirely notional) asset value placed on expertise and the speed with which it might become a liability, especially if circumstances change.

It is also possible to see assets as having short-, medium- and long-term value. Those assets that are regarded as having long-term value must always be seen in the context that they may have to be written off from an investment (if not accounting) point of view if circumstances suddenly change, or if the expertise or technology suddenly becomes obsolete.

LIABILITIES

Liabilities are the obligations and charges that are certain to be incurred as a result of the activities created by the venture. These can be described as:

- Regular and continuing costs and obligations, including: interest charges; staff costs and charges; administration; premises and technology charges.
- Activity-related charges which vary according to the nature of the venture. The most universal are marketing, maintenance, research and development; as well as charges incurred through the density, frequency and value of activities.
- Short-term liabilities incurred, for example, by hiring extra or specialised expertise or equipment to get over a particular problem and for which a long-term benefit is expected to accrue.
- Intangible liabilities of which the most common is the development of a bad reputation based on poor production quality and volume; inability to meet deadlines; poor presentation.
- Sudden liabilities which occur as the result of sudden obsolescence of technology or expertise.

THE RELATIONSHIP BETWEEN ASSETS AND LIABILITIES

From an accounting point of view, a relationship can be established between each designated asset and liability through comparisons and ratio analysis (see below).

When appraising investments, a broader perspective is required. Something that is bought in as an asset can turn quickly into a liability. Production and information technology, bought as a long-term investment, may be rendered obsolete at any time by new inventions. Building companies that buy up land banks find that these become a liability if the demand for buildings dries up, if the price of land falls, or if the political perspective on construction work changes. Projects for which capital goods have been bought may be cancelled if other costs or unforeseen problems make the project no longer viable. A piece of equipment that can produce 5000 items per year for a designated useful life of 10 years may have to be scrapped and written off altogether if a new and better machine becomes available after

two years. Those with expertise become liabilities if they are able to charge
fees for their services that are greater than the returns available to the
venture; particular experts may also lose their reputation and employability
if they become embroiled in personal scandal.

Ratio Analysis

Ratio analyses are used by accountants to identify, establish and measure
the relationships and performance aspects of a stated asset against a stated
liability. From this, it is possible to establish particular aspects of financial
information (Figure 2.3).

Ratio calculation provides distinctive measures of particular activities.
The information gained has to be seen in context, however. For example,
while a quick ratio may show that a company could not easily cover its
current liabilities, if these are not to be called in, this does not matter.

Similarly, the debtors and creditors ratio may show that a particular
company is damaging its own cash flow by paying its bills more quickly than
it receives payments. However, if this is the sectoral norm, then it may be
able to do little about this.

Profit ratio $\dfrac{\text{Net profit}}{\text{Total sales}} \times 100$ Indicates percentage return

Selling costs $\dfrac{\text{Selling costs}}{\text{Total sales}} \times 100$ Indicates percentage consumed on sales costs

The same approach can be taken for energy, production, marketing, staff, distribution,
research, development and capital goods as a percentage of sales.

Assets and Liabilities $\dfrac{\text{Assets}}{\text{Liabilities}}$ A general ready-reckoner

This may then be broken down into:

(a) $\dfrac{\text{Long-term assets}}{\text{Long-term liabilities}}$

(b) $\dfrac{\text{Current assets}}{\text{Current liabilities}}$

(c) A quick ratio or 'the acid test' which is

$$\dfrac{\text{Quickly realisable assets including cash}}{\text{Current liabilities}}$$

(d) Debtors and creditors $\dfrac{\text{Debtors}}{\text{Creditors}}$ Indicates whether an organisation is paying out its bills more quickly than it is receiving payments

Figure 2.3   *Ratio analyses*

Assets have both an accounting value and a real value. Thus an item of technology priced at £100,000 that is being written off at £20,000 per annum for five years has a residual asset value of £60,000 after two years. However, if the equipment has suddenly become obsolete as the result of inventions and developments, it is likely that the equipment will have to be scrapped. Property and premises values have also to be seen in the same way. When it is known and understood that property and premises are to be divested, the price that can be charged for their sale always falls. This again is in spite of the value placed on it by accounting and financial inventions. The difference between property values and the ability to command prices based on those values is at its narrowest when either the property itself commands an economic rent, normally based on its location; or the company selling the property is able to wait until the right price is achieved.

RETURNS ON INVESTMENT AND RETURNS ON CAPITAL EMPLOYED

Calculating returns on investment and returns on capital employed is overtly straightforward. The formula is as follows.

$$\frac{\text{Income generated}}{\text{Investment/capital employed}} \times 100 = \text{Percentage rate of return}$$

Problems arise with this, however, if the capital employed in the venture is not precisely defined, or if the real level or value of the investment to all parties concerned is not understood. This is exacerbated by promised and 'certain' predicted rates of return, which often come to be accepted as 'the truth' as the result of the barriers and assumptions indicated above, and as the result of calculations carried out and analysed from a narrow perspective only.

Real and projected rates of return are also distorted when resources from outside the direct investment are used in pursuing it, but then not included in the return on investment or capital employed calculations. It is necessary to distinguish between gross and net return on investment and return on capital employed; while it is usual to present this as net, whichever is the case needs to be made clear.

There may also be derived returns, and these can be both positive and negative. From a positive point of view, this is the enhancement of reputation, better than anticipated returns, and the opportunity to pursue new ventures. Negative rates of return include provision for bad debt, loss of reputation, unsuccessful ventures, or changes in priorities that have taken place during the course of completion of the project.

Returns on investment calculations may also be subject to time constraints, especially the pressures of the annual report. This, again, is the
particular problem in long-term ventures, where, because of the nature of
the investment made, shareholders may not receive anticipated dividends or
the desired level of increase in the value of their shares.

Expected and anticipated returns on investment and on capital employed
reflect the nature and extent of expectations and anticipations of shareholders, other backers, stakeholders and vested interests. Managerial approaches to projections of returns therefore tend towards the lowest
common denominator because anything above this is normally perceived
to be over-successful.

Calculating returns on capital employed is most useful as comparator
between desired and actual performance. This should provide a key point of
enquiry when evaluating the success or failure of activities and ventures. It
may also identify particular inefficiencies of resource utilisation. Others will
look at inflation, interest and retail price indices as a general benchmark on
which to assess their returns for basic acceptability.

Returns on capital employed should always be seen in terms of the nature
of actual returns in the particular industrial, commercial or public service
sector in question.

Returns on investment must also be seen in terms of the size and value of
the particular venture, and of the other opportunities available. For
example, if taken in isolation, simply carrying out the calculations without
consideration of the broader context, might lead a venturer to conclude that
a 15 per cent return on £1,000 over a five-year period was more attractive
than a 14 per cent return on £5,000 over a twenty-year period.

NET PRESENT VALUES

The net present value of an investment can be defined as 'the value today of
the surplus that the company makes, over the future period of time that the
surplus is made'.

This is based on two considerations:

1. that the company has assessed its lowest acceptable rate of return on
    investment;
2. that the investment itself has a better or more assured chance of
    achieving that rate of return than the next most overtly profitable
    venture available.

This may be summarised by the formula shown in Figure 2.4.

Provided that the information fed into the formula is based on real
research and venture assessment, and that contextual and situational factors

have been taken into account, the calculation provides a useful indication of likely rates of return. The calculation can then be carried out for best, medium and worst outcomes (see Figure 2.5).

While this provides a measure of substantial quantitative information on which investment decisions can be taken, the problem lies in the fact that anything in between the two extremes indicated will nevertheless become acceptable. In other words, provided any form of positive outcome to the venture can be envisaged, the decision is likely to be taken to go ahead with it. The medium-acceptable rate of return envisaged may then become a point at which inefficiencies and ineffectiveness present in the inception and completion of the venture are not fully considered because the overall rates of return are well within the margins of acceptability.

$$\text{Net present value} = \frac{A}{1+R} + \frac{A}{(1+R)^2} + \frac{A}{(1+R)^3} + \cdots\cdots + \frac{A}{(1+R)^n} - I$$

Where:

A = the net cash flow in the particular year
n = the point in time when the project comes to the end of its life, representing the total number of years in which the project has been conducted
R = the firm's annual rate of discount
I = the initial cost of the investment

Figure 2.4   *Net present value formula*

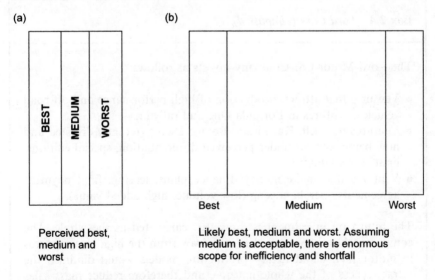

(a)   Perceived best, medium and worst

(b)   Likely best, medium and worst. Assuming medium is acceptable, there is enormous scope for inefficiency and shortfall

Different projections of net present value can then be plotted on the box

Figure 2.5   *Best, medium and worst outcomes*

Net present value calculations may also be used to assess the relative merits of continuing ventures and activities. They can be used to analyse products and service portfolios in terms of:

- those which attract investment; those which attract buyer and consumer interest;
- those which people buy, which contribute to particular volumes of sales as a percentage of the total;
- those on which the greatest margins are achieved; those on which the greatest margins can be projected.

It also provides a calculated assessment of those ventures that are coming to the end of their useful life; and those on which the desired or required rates of return are no longer forthcoming. This is likely to provide a basis for discussion as to whether particular products, projects and ventures should be continued or divested.

Again, however, this has to be seen in the broadest context. In particular, the attract/sell/make money approach needs to be seen as a whole rather than as parts. For example, the divestment of a product or venture which is attractive but does not produce returns must be seen in terms of the knock-on effects that it may have on the rest of the activities (see box 2.4).

Box 2.4 *Ford Cars (simplified)*

The Ford Motor Car Company invests as follows:

- Ventures that attract: production of high performance and off-road vehicles; ventures in Formula One and rallying.
- Ventures that sell: Ka, Fiesta, Bonus; Escort (recently divested and now being sold off under perceived differentiation, special editions, limited availability).
- Ventures that make money: finance plans, leasing, final payment agreements; merchandising (low volume, high added value).

The return on investment is, however, calculated as the whole. The company takes the view that to withdraw from the high cost ventures in motor racing and luxury production models would diminish the attractiveness of the whole marque, and therefore reduce mass sales and the finance plans that go with these.

COST BENEFIT ANALYSIS

Cost benefit analysis is a quick and easy ready-reckoner method of establishing a basis on which a given initiative might be feasible or profitable (in whatever terms that may be measured), and of identifying those elements that require further more detailed consideration before it is implemented. It simply requires itemising all the costs and charges that could possibly be incurred in the venture, and setting them against all the values and benefits that the completed item, project or product might bring.

Cost benefit analysis is used widely in the consideration of public sector projects, and those commercial ventures that bring with them real or perceived social benefits. Cost benefit analysis involves consideration of nine related areas (see Figure 2.6).

The approach is as follows:

- *Action choices:* the meaning of the costs and benefits of alternative courses of action in relation to each other.
- *Time frames:* short-, medium- and long-term – the time periods over which costs are to be incurred; and which the results and benefits are to be measured. Consideration is also given at this point to the period over which they are required by investors and backers, and other vested interests.
- *Values:* values that are seen from both the economic and income generation point of view, and also in wider terms, of public acceptance and benefit, so that a social benefit can be assessed.
- *Priorities:* the priorities ascribed by all involved to the particular undertaking; where the venture lies in the order of priority of all those involved; and what opportunities might have to be forgone by some of those involved.

ACTION CHOICES	PRIORITIES	INITIATIVES
TIME FRAME SHORT MEDIUM LONG-TERM	STRATEGIC ASPECTS	RISK
RELATIVE VALUATION	INCOME EXPENDITURE	VALUE

Figure 2.6 Cost benefit analysis model

- *Initiatives:* with especial reference to the effect that particular ventures might have in terms of derived income and wealth generation; and also to less acceptable by-products such as effluent, waste and environmental damage.
- *Risk and uncertainty:* consideration of the aspects of risk must be built in to this form of evaluation of any venture.
- *Strategy:* strategic aspects and overview will take account of all aspects of political, economic and social costs and benefits as well as the direct financial demands and implications presented.
- *Relativity:* the relative valuation of different costs and benefits in terms of all those involved in the venture; in terms of the frequency and intervals at which they occur; and how to reconcile these when they occur at different points in time, or in relation to the different priorities brought by all those concerned to the venture.
- *Income and expenditure:* related in particular to values that accrue to those on different incomes; those dependent on the completion of the venture for continued employment; questions of political, and other, reputation and enhancement.

Cost benefit analysis has normally been used as one key method of assessing the viability of public and politically driven projects and initiatives.

It is, however, of increasing importance that commercial ventures consider their investments – especially large and long-term projects – from this broader perspective, because of legal constraints continually being imposed in matters of employment protection, and environmental awareness and responsibility. Those seeking to become involved in private finance initiative ventures, and the delivery of services hitherto part of the public domain, also need to consider the cost benefit perspective if they are to fully understand the situation in which they are being asked to operate in the future. The following are examples of this (see Figures 2.7, 2.8 and 2.9).

Each venture can be seen in this way from the narrow perspective of maximising investment, or the broader perspective of accepting the responsibilities and consequences of that investment. This will not necessarily mean that those involved will not proceed purely from the narrow point of view. However, it does indicate some of the obligations and responsibilities inherent in different types of venture; it also indicates the fact that eventually someone will be called to account for these.

From each point of view there is a moral question to be addressed. This comes in three forms.

(1) *Moral pricing*: This has especial reference to the third example, where the children might be perceived as being the commodity output of the venture, on which charges and income are accrued. The balance here will be between what the public bodies responsible for placing the

ACTION CHOICE	PRIORITY	INITIATIVE
• size • capacity	• policy-driven • vested interests • motoring and transport lobbies	• integrated transport or isolated scheme • job creation
LONG-TERM • usage	STRATEGIC ASPECT • to shift traffic problem *or* to solve traffic problem	RISK • low, provided finance is available • materials usage
RELATIVE VALUATION by: (a) government as a whole (b) Department of Transport (c) user	INCOME–EXPENDITURE • income only from tolls, or as the result of increased volumes of traffic • no direct return otherwise	VALUE • to users • negative value to environmental and social lobbies

Figure 2.7 Cost benefit analysis model for a motorway scheme

ACTION CHOICE	PRIORITY	INITIATIVE
• size • capacity • projected length of useful life • resale value	• buy/lease • construct	• market aimed at • ability and propensity to pay
SHORT-TERM • familiarity, confidence LONG-TERM • market size	STRATEGY • niche • competition from other holiday packages • returns on volume sales	RISK • local publicity • accidents and tragedies both to this venture and others would cause loss of overall confidence and demand
RELATIVE VALUATION • low to consumers, part of very high choice sector	INCOME • steady, long-term EXPENDITURE • high initial • steady long-term	VALUE • ability to brand and differentiate • perceived value

Figure 2.8 Cost benefit analysis model for a cruise liner

Investment Appraisal

ACTION CHOICE	PRIORITY	INITIATIVE
• to privatise	• to reduce public expenditure(!) • to offer choice(!) • Political and expedient	• to address a long-term social and political problem
SHORT-TERM • responsibility is removed from public service LONG-TERM • problem remains	STRATEGY • part of wider privatisation policy • part of wider social policy • not fully defined	RISK • political: high, due to scandals, abuse, abuses, overcharging contractor can unilaterally pull out
RELATIVE VALUATION • low – problems like this are under-invested and undervalued	INCOME • to contractor: high, economic rent EXPENDITURE • no public capital expenditure • charges are high	VALUE • social problems and clients as commodities

Figure 2.9 *Cost benefit analysis model for a privatised children's home*

children would like to pay (low), what they can pay (high), and what the private venturer would like to charge (high), but with the caveat that they might receive unacceptable press coverage, and social revulsion, through maximising the potential charges.

(2) *Expediency*: This is a feature of each of the examples given. A by-product of public capital works such as the motorway scheme is always to create fresh employment, and this may be politically expedient in areas of high unemployment, or in the run-up to elections. The cruise liner may choose to sail to places where unregulated dumping of effluent is carried out by others involved in the sector; or to where high profits can be accrued as the result of sailing to perceived exotic, but in fact extremely cheap, locations. The children's home venture is also attractive from this point of view, because it removes a problem from the public domain in the short term, in return for a cash payment.

(3) *Environmental effects*: both the inception of the venture, and also the end-usage, bring with them environmental effects that hitherto have not necessarily been considered a key part of any cost benefit analysis. Construction projects bring urban environmental noise, lighting and

other pollution and waste blight. The travel and tourism industry consumes large quantities of packaging, energy, fossil fuels, as well as imposing its own conditions on the places that it visits. This form of privatisation of public services also incurs residual environmental building and construction activities; and may also incur 'social blight' – where other members of the community do not wish to have the particular venture located near them. While this may indicate a lack of moral fibre, those in the area looking after their own narrow self interest may nevertheless point to real or perceived reductions in property values, and real or perceived questions of security or acceptability, in support of their case.

THE MULTIPLIER

The multiplier model is as shown in Figure 2.10. The multiplier model assumes that when investment is made in one activity, beneficiaries of that investment will spend a certain amount of their benefits accrued. It also assumes that they will not spend it all.

It is extensively used as the basis for public capital projects to generate employment, prosperity, and therefore further commercial activities in certain areas. More recently, it has been used by sports goods and clothing manufacturing companies in hitherto unindustrialised parts of the Third World, and those dependent upon Western investment for improvements in prosperity and quality of life. However, this has led to allegations of exploitation and corporate racketeering. In one case in Pakistan, it was found that balls were being made for international football tournaments by children as young as six; in another, high quality trainers retailing for £149.99 were being made in sweat shops in Haiti by people earning the equivalent of 30 pence per day for a 15-hour day. In each case, the protagonists argued that they were bringing additional prosperity to the particular locations, and thus contributing to economic development.

Investment $\longrightarrow$ Reinvestment $\longrightarrow$ Reinvestment $\longrightarrow$ Reinvestment $\cdots\cdots$

Putting a financial figure in place of the investment, the process can be modelled as follows.

(a) Assuming 50% onward expenditure:

£1,000 $\longrightarrow$ £500 $\longrightarrow$ £250 $\longrightarrow$ £125 $\longrightarrow$ £62.50 $\longrightarrow$ $\cdots\cdots$

(b) Assuming 25% onward expenditure:

£1,000 $\longrightarrow$ £250 $\longrightarrow$ £62.50 $\longrightarrow$ £15.62 $\longrightarrow$ $\cdots\cdots$

Figure 2.10 *The multiplier model*

The multiplier may also be seen as:

- *The accelerator*: In order to gain credibility, support and recognition for a particular venture, it may be necessary to get it off the ground, and to have demonstrable tangible results quickly; this is a particular feature of urban and dockland renewal programmes in the UK, and as a consequence initial investments had to be underwritten by UK government, thus making it as attractive as possible to draw in the level of resources necessary to achieve the initial aims.
- *The decelerator*: When there is an under-assessment of the multiplier effect, unsustainable short-term economic mini-booms are likely to take place. In the short term this leads to the overvaluation of property, expertise, technology and other perceived assets; and this may, in turn, lead to cost- and demand-led inflation.

The decelerator is therefore engaged. This normally takes the form of:

(1) Informal government lobbying of venturers and major backers to ask them to slow down particular investment processes;
(2) Increases in interest rates and restraints placed on the finance industry in terms of where it may invest its money.

The normal output of the decelerator is to reduce confidence, and therefore capital and consumer expenditure. In recent years, it has also led to the accumulation of large volumes of consumer and capital debts, especially in terms of the inability to sustain and service property values and charges.

CONCLUSIONS

The models and instruments indicated in this chapter enable much more informed and accurate approaches to investment decisions to be taken. Whichever of the approaches are used, the essential output is as follows.

- The levels of return that the sector is providing at the moment
- The levels of return that the sector may be expected to provide in the future
- The levels of return desired by those involved
- Pay-back periods on particular activities and sub-activities
- Identification and evaluation of alternatives available to ventures and the uses to which resources might be put
- The cost structure and mixes of particular sectors
- The risk structure and mixes of a particular sector (see Chapter 7).

The purpose of gathering, assessing and evaluating data using these particular approaches is to provide a sound basis for taking effective, successful and profitable investment decisions. The techniques indicated only provide the basis for this judgement and evaluation; they do not constitute judgement and evaluation. At best, they indicate the fundamental soundness or otherwise of proposals, and some of the consequences that are likely to occur if particular decisions are taken. They indicate key points of enquiry, and potential opportunities, issues and problems. Whether it is worth pursuing a particular venture is down to the expertise and quality with which the information is judged, evaluated and used.

3 Strategy, Policy and Direction in Investment Appraisal

INTRODUCTION

Investment strategy, policy and direction are drawn up for the purpose of establishing:

- what is being invested in and why
- when the investment is to take place
- how the investment is to be managed
- the returns that are required and that are expected to accrue
- the place and priority of the particular venture in the context of the rest of the organisation's activities.

This applies both to those making investments and to those proposing ventures, projects and initiatives. If these questions are addressed effectively at the inception of any venture, project or proposal, the outcomes are:

- clarity of purpose and direction, understood and accepted by all those involved
- compatibility of purpose among all those involved
- simplicity and directness of purpose, capable of being understood and accepted by all those subsequently involved, including staff, customers, future backers and end-users
- confidence in the venture or initiative in question on the part of all involved
- ability to achieve commitment to purpose and therefore effective implementation.

As stated in Chapter 1, for this to be effective, extensive and effective groundwork needs to be carried out. In order to do this, an understanding of the process required is essential (see box 3.1).

Box 3.1 *What the strategy process is not*

The strategy process is not any of the following.

- Bland or general statements of purpose that, in fact, bind nobody to anything.
- Use of the words 'synergy' or 'economies of scale' without precise definitions of what these are in the particular situation, or how these are to be achieved.
- Media sound bites: while the presentation of investment purpose or direction may have to be delivered in terms acceptable to the media, at the core of the proposal there must exist solid foundations on which the sound bite or media story was delivered.
- Anything that involves 'seeking', 'hoping', or 'expecting' to achieve anything. Returns on investment are not achieved through adopting any of the attitudes expressed or implicit in these words.

FOUNDATIONS OF STRATEGY, POLICY AND DIRECTION

Porter (1982) defines three core generic positions as the foundation for all successful ventures as follows.

- *Cost leadership*: Cost leadership is where the organisation concentrates on being the lowest-cost operator in its sector. In order to be able to do this, it seeks out all sources of cost advantage. Companies that pursue this approach concentrate their investment on high-quality, enduring production and service technology, and high-quality and enduring technical and professional expertise to ensure that it is exploited to the full. Financial returns on investment, where a cost leadership strategy is followed, depend on the difference between the levels of investment required to secure cost advantage, and the price or charges that can be made for the products, services or ventures so delivered. Where it is possible to charge premium prices, there is the clear prospect of high margins and high levels of sustainable long-term financial success and performance.
- *Focus*: Focus strategy occurs when organisations concentrate on specific segments within a sector and then seek to serve them to the exclusion of all others. Investment here is concerned with concentration on identifying, anticipating and meeting the needs of the segment and ensuring that this is accurately completed. Technology and expertise in the service of a narrow segment is likely to be specialist and concentrated. If, at any point,

expansion becomes desirable or required, the most effective way to secure a return on investment is to seek further outlets for existing products or services, rather than diversifying into new technology and expertise requirements.

- *Differentiation*: Differentiation strategies are those that seek a perceived uniqueness or identity for their products in ways that are widely valued by buyers other than price advantage. This involves marketing, promotions, packaging and public relations activities to give both the venture itself, and also any outputs, a distinctive identity. Organisations that can achieve and sustain differentiation gain their return on investment, provided that the price premium more than covers the costs and charges incurred in *being different*.

There are direct implications for investment ventures.

Cost Leadership

Sustainable cost leadership and cost advantage requires continued attention to, and investment in, the technology and skills required (see above). There is a clear potential conflict between financiers and managers here. For example, investment in equipment may be made on the basis that it has a useful working life of three years, and output costs, depreciation and write-off are calculated over that period. However, in order to sustain commercial production and cost advantage, it is necessary to replace the equivalent immediately an alternative becomes available that can do the job quicker or better.

Similarly, from the point of view of the investor, cost advantages are sustained by moving funds into those areas where they will produce the best long-term sustainable returns. This is not so much of a problem when attracting institutional backing, but it is when the backer's resources are limited (see box 3.2).

The emphasis needs to be placed on the level of funding necessary to achieve and sustain long-term cost advantage. Accounting mechanisms therefore need to be devised with this in mind rather than designing investment strategy to fit in with existing accounts' policies and practices. It also points to the need for mutual confidence and effective relations between all those involved in any venture or initiative.

Focus

Investment is concerned with ensuring density and effectiveness of niche coverage. It is again important to stress that this must be capable of accommodation from all points of view. Those who invest in narrow niches and specialist sectors must understand the need for flexibility and

---

Box 3.2 *Cost leaders: examples*

- *UK cars*: The cost leader in the UK car industry is Nissan. The investment required to sustain this consists of: adequate flexible production technology, systematically maintained; full flexibility of staff training (the initial training costs per member of staff are in the order of £10,000 each); guarantees of lifetime employment, provided that full flexibility of working is accepted; attention to the quality of the working environment; no strike arrangements with the workforce; the highest levels of pay in the UK car sector. In return for this, the company finds itself able to sustain the widest cost price margins of any manufacturer within the European Union, and to compete on price according to local market conditions.
- *Air travel*: EasyJet is the cost leader in the UK air industry. This is achieved through concentrating the investment priorities on frontline service delivery, good quality reliable aircraft, and popular short-haul routes. The company overhead is kept to a minimum. Staffing priorities are concerned with ensuring above average (though not the best for the sector) wage levels, combined with extensive staff training for those directly concerned with the public. A major part of the investment in this company's cost leadership is concerned with gaining greater public acceptance and recognition for the use of Edinburgh, Manchester, Stansted, Luton and Manston airports as convenient and well-recognised points of departure from the UK.
- *Groceries*: In the UK, Tesco is the cost leader (though this may change when WalMart become fully operational in the Year 2003). The return on investment is measured in terms of: frequency and density of store usage; returns per square metre; and returns per product and product cluster. For this to be effective, investment must concentrate on having the floor space, variety and diversity of products available to sustain the reality and perception of universal customer choice. Great attention is also paid to store layout, to try and ensure that customers make as many on-the-spot, unconsidered purchases as possible; however, these are seen as windfall or peripheral, rather than core, components of business.

Attention is drawn to the levels and length of investment implicit in each of these examples. None of these is a short-term venture, nor could the levels of investment required to be a cost leader in each of these areas be contemplated if they were so.

responsiveness; and for frequency and density of operation within the niche. This, above all, includes the provision for emergency, contingency and short-term funds so that opportunities that do become apparent along the way can be exploited.

This also applies to capital project work in the construction, engineering and technology sectors. Those who invest in these highly specialised areas need to understand the full context of the work rather than concentrating on the perceived certainty of returns at the end (see box 3.3).

Box 3.3 *Sock Shop*

Sock Shop was founded in 1980 by Sophie Mirman. The venture was based on providing a convenient point of access for those requiring socks, ties and underwear – unconsidered items of clothing that people would not normally go out of their way to buy. Extensive and effective market research concluded that the best way for the investment to go forward was to open small shops on the major railway stations of London and other large cities in the UK. The niche served would therefore be the daily travelling public, with peaks of business in the morning and evening rush hours.

The venture was very successful, achieving turnover of £28 million within three years of opening, and a return on investment of 350 per cent over the same period.

The company sought other outlets for its existing products. Consequently, it took the venture to the railway stations of the big cities of North America. However, it totally failed to understand consumer and end-user behaviour in those places. There, consumers were neither used to making purchases of this nature at the beginning or end of railway journeys, nor confident doing so (because of real and perceived criminal activities in those places). The company lost most of its investment in these ventures when they were forced to close. It then compounded the error by trying to diversify in its existing locations, therefore losing its distinctive identity – focus – with its customers. The venture went bankrupt in 1991.

Differentiation

The major requirement here is for a steady stream of funds for application to all aspects of differentiating products and services, and to have these available whenever required. Specific aspects for which such funds are necessary are performance, design, image, marketing, packaging, advertising and promotion.

Some of this, based on the organisation's own initiatives, can be predicted and therefore planned for. However, a key feature of effective differentiation is the ability to respond to competitor's initiatives, and provision for this has to be built in. This, in turn, may lead to increases in anticipated or predicted levels of investment. These are required either to sustain price wars, or to increase advertising, presentation and packaging expenditure. It is also necessary to recognise the uncertainties of each, and to include the funding of failure (see box 3.4).

Box 3.4   *Differentiation failures*

Examples are as follows.

- *Abbey National plc*: The Abbey National is a leading UK high street bank. As a Building Society, for 20 years it sustained its identity on the slogan 'The Abbey Habit'. Supported with bright sunny images, this helped to ensure that the customer base of the company grew from 1.5 million in the mid-1960s to 9.5 million in the late 1980s. However, the company felt the need to modernise and changed its slogan to 'Abbey Endings'. This was intended to be a play on the phrase 'Happy Endings' – i.e. that the bank's customers would live happily ever after. However, potential customers saw not the word *happy* but the word *endings* – and therefore were being faced with their own mortality. This was unacceptable; and the bank failed to attract the desired volume of new customers. The venture was cancelled after 18 months.
- *Sony*: In the late 1960s, the Sony Corporation invented the Betamax video system. It was superior in operation to the VHS system that was beginning to come into wide usage and the company perceived that superior Betamax product reliability and quality of pictures would cause the VHS system to be dropped by others. This failed because of the wideness of availability of VHS-based products; and that competitors were able to compete on price for the video cassette recorders and players. Sony cancelled the venture in 1975, though they redeemed a good part of the investment by using the technology that had been discovered to give them a quality and cost advantage when entering into film and television programme production upon their acquisition of Columbia-Tristar Pictures.

- *Fashion Café*: The Fashion Café was opened in Leicester Square, London, at the beginning of 1997. Its perceived uniqueness was given to it through the backing of the supermodels Naomi Campbell, Elle MacPherson, Kate Moss and Eva Herzigova. In the eyes of the proprietors, this gave it a perceived uniqueness and exclusivity. Customers would be driven by association to use the café and, surrounded by pictures of the supermodels, be prepared to pay premium prices. In practice, many customers went once to see what all the fuss was about, and then, faced with the extremely high prices, would go elsewhere in future. The perceived product quality was not sufficient to encourage people to return for subsequent visits. They perceived that, apart from the association with the supermodels, the product was no different to that available at lesser prices elsewhere in London; and that greater satisfaction would be afforded by going to alternatives. The venture closed in June 1999.

Porter's hypothesis is that all effective competitive strategies must start from a clear position of cost advantage, focus, or differentiation, and that it is essential that everyone concerned is clear about which it is, if success is to be achieved. However, it is clear that:

- There are plenty of perceived acceptable performers among those companies whose strategies are not clearly defined from one of these points of view (see box 3.5).
- There are plenty of organisations that have clearly defined strategy but cannot sustain themselves long-term (see box 3.6).
- There are plenty of performers that do not have a clearly defined strategy that have either drifted, or else subsequently been forced to reposition themselves (see box 3.7).

At the very least, this form of approach helps to establish the point of view from which the particular venture is designed and received, and enables an initial understanding of what all of the parties may reasonably expect as a result. This then leads to more detailed analysis.

Social, Technical, Economic, Political: STEP Analysis

The purpose of this analysis is to help organisations assess the broad environment in which investments and ventures are to take place. Those involved carry out a brainstorming exercise under the headings of social, technological, economic and political factors (see Figures 3.1 and 3.2).

Social	Technological
• Population • Lifestyle • Spending patterns • Social attitudes and values • Prejudices • Social segmentation	• Education and training • Technological advance and invention • Obsolescence • Potential • Energy usage
Economic	Political
• Confidence • Spending patterns • Propensity to spend • Inflation • Interest rates • Value of currencies • Fixed and variable costs	• Government stance • Environmental issues • Political pressures • Sector regulation • Legal factors • Acceptability

Figure 3.1 *STEP analysis model*

Social	Technological
• Expected returns (very tenuous) • Political pressures • Perceptions: 'You will be poor if you don't' • Responsibility • Can I afford it?	• Some idea (?) of value of investment • Access to benefits
Economic	Political
• Interest rates • Inflation rates • Decline in public benefits and social security • Uncertainties of European Union policies in the area	• Political emphases • Drives towards personal not state responsibilities • Encouraging self-sufficiency

Note:
The result of this analysis is largely to highlight general points and issues that need much greater investigation.

Figure 3.2 *Example: STEP analysis for personal investment proposals*

Box 3.5   *Market and sector dominance*

Large, diverse and dominant companies are able to sustain a competitive position in the medium to long-term provided that they recognise that any inefficiencies in-built have to be managed. Examples of companies enjoying such positions are:

- British Airways (air travel) is able to dominate its sector because of its command of routes and landing slots, and because the competitors are sufficiently small only to be able to compete on specific routes;
- Thomas Cook (travel agency and services) is able to dominate its sector through offering a variety of travel and tour packages, convenient but expensive currency exchange facilities, and convenient but expensive travel insurance arrangements;
- Department stores such as Boots and Debenhams are able to sustain competitive advantage because, while they are not cost leaders in the sector, the product range is sufficiently specialised to attract medium to long term commercially viable clients, customers and end-users, even though their products are available at other outlets. Boots also enjoys market dominance in cosmetics, baby goods, and retail pharmaceutical sectors.

Box 3.6   *The problems of being a niche operator*

- BMW are a top-of-the-range motorcycle and motor car manufacturer; and they also make and sell aircraft engines. They are extremely highly regarded in the niches that they serve. However, in 1997 the company found itself having to acquire a mass-market car manufacturer in order to generate sufficient volume of sales to sustain the high quality activities on a commercial basis.
- Body Shop, the high-quality organic cosmetics retailer, has found itself having to reposition or differentiate itself in this sector. This is because larger and more established players have introduced their own range of substitute goods at competitive prices. The company has sought to diversify into ornaments, other products from elsewhere in the world, perfumes and fragrances, in order to try and enlarge its customer base.

Box 3.7   *The declining market share of Sainsbury*

In 1986 Sainsbury's enjoyed a position of being the largest grocery retailer and supermarket chain in the UK. It had 20 per cent of the market and more stores than anyone else. The next largest player at the time was Tesco with 11 per cent of the market.

In 1999 the position had almost reversed, with Sainsbury's down to 11 per cent of market share, while Tesco enjoyed 18 per cent.

Also in 1986, David Sainsbury, the then Chairman of Sainsbury's, took part in a television discussion with Michael Porter. In this discussion, Porter pointed out the potential weakness of Sainsbury's strategic position. This, David Sainsbury had described as: 'making superior profits, if at the same time you can keep costs down, and have prices which are competitive, and get tremendous turnover. Then you get cost advantages which enable you to actually make superior profits without commanding a premium price, because you can have the lower price'. At the time, Sainsbury's were able to sustain their superior competitive position and market dominance largely on the basis of their physical size. On the basis of David Sainsbury's statement, no clear strategic position had been adopted. Neither was any attention paid to the inefficiencies inherent in this position.

Source: M. E. Porter, *The World Turned Upside Down*, Channel 4
Television, 1986.

Strengths, Weaknesses, Opportunities, Threats: SWOT Analysis

The purpose of conducting a SWOT analysis is to help organisations to learn, to clarify issues, to identify preferred and likely directions, and to conduct a general and quick analysis of the potential of particular ventures. It is likely to throw up specific issues that have then to be further analysed and evaluated.

In SWOT analyses, issues are raised, highlighted and categorised (see Figures 3.3 and 3.4).

Competitor Analysis

Competitor analysis involves assessing other potential sources of, or targets for, investment. This includes initiatives that may be taken to promote the position of competitors; or to promote ventures that may cause other

STRENGTHS	WEAKNESSES
• Name • Reputation • Financial strength • Public confidence • Confidence of other venturers	• Customer complaints • Product recalls • Skilled staff shortages • Technology shortages • Dominance–dependency • Inefficiencies
• Consequences of failure • Consequences of success • Future technological invention • Opportunity costs (ventures which may subsequently become apparent)	• Growth • Familiarity • Technological advance • Market development • Acquisition
THREATS	OPPORTUNITIES

Figure 3.3   *SWOT analysis model*

STRENGTHS	WEAKNESSES
• Command of supplies • Certainty of production and output • Certainty of supply pricing and charges	• Affordability • Potential for substitution and alternatives • Suppliers may not want to be taken over
• Long-term affordability • Threat of substitution • Residual value if supplies become obsolete • Inability to command prices for supplies	• Certainty of supply • Potential to sell supplies elsewhere • Value of supplier's other assets (and liabilities)
THREATS	OPPORTUNITIES

Note:
The balance of strengths and opportunities, weaknesses and threats, as the basis for *managerial* judgement.

Figure 3.4   *Example: SWOT analysis model for taking over a major supplier*

competitors to enter the market. It is also necessary to be able to measure the likely responses of those involved to such proposals and initiatives.

The components of a competitor analysis are as shown in Figures 3.5, 3.6 and 3.7. By addressing each of these five points, and the ways in which they interrelate and interact, informed conclusions can be arrived at under the following headings.

- The strategy of the competitor
- Competitor's driving and restraining forces
- Competitor's current operations and ventures, capacities and strengths
- Competitor's current levels of confidence, reputation and image, and the basis on which these are arrived at
- Testing, evaluating and researching, where necessary, assumptions held about the competitor
- Testing, evaluating and researching, where necessary, assumptions held about the whole sector.

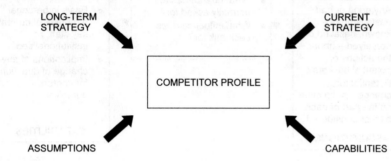

Figure 3.5   *The components of a competitor analysis*

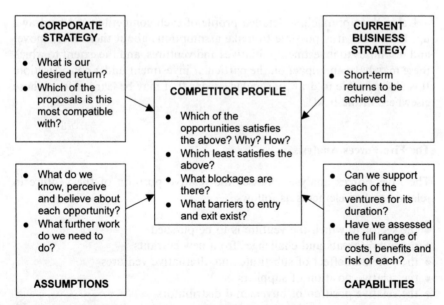

Figure 3.6   *Example: competitor analysis for a corporate investor seeking to place funds*

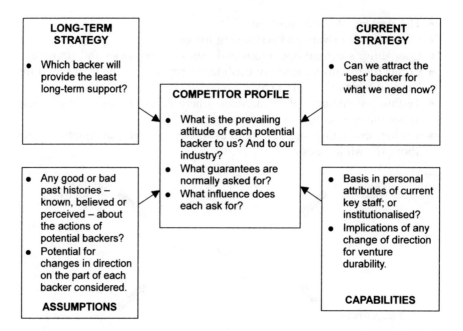

Figure 3.7 *Example: competitor analysis for a small specialist engineering company
seeking to attract funds for expansion*

Using this approach, a detailed profile of each competitor can be drawn
up. From this, it is possible to make assumptions about their likely moves
and responses to investment initiatives and ventures, and the extent to which
these may have an impact on the particular investment under consideration.
It is also possible to draw particular lessons that may be learned from those
elsewhere in the field.

The Five Forces Analysis

The Five Forces analysis assesses the relative position of the venture in
relation to five elements as follows:

- the sector in which the venture is to be pursued
- potential threats and challenges from new entrants
- the potential effect of substitute and alternative ventures
- the relative position of suppliers
- the relative position of buyers and distributors.

It is presented diagrammatically as shown in Figures 3.8 and 3.9.

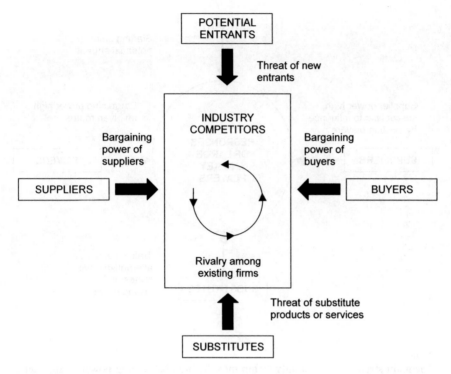

Figure 3.8 *Five Forces model*

Of particular concern to investors are the supply and substitute areas. Investors need to be satisfied that their money is not going to be either over-concentrated on securing and stockpiling supplies, or else used for fighting off competition from other sources. They also need to be satisfied that their money is not going to be lost as a result of inability to secure supplies, and/ or as a result of the market drying up because of the emergence of alternatives and substitutes for the particular venture.

Customer and End-User Analysis

The basis of effective customer and end-user analysis lies in identifying the following elements:

- *Characteristics*: personal and professional characteristics; their general and particular levels of expectation.
- *Priorities*: their real priorities; their own perceptions of their priorities.
- *Needs and wants*: and especially being able to distinguish between the two.

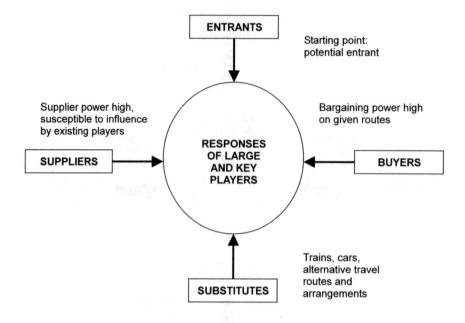

Note:
The main strength is the ability to tap into the high bargaining power of suppliers. The other aspects constitute major barriers to entry.

Figure 3.9   *Example: Five Forces analysis for a low-cost, good-value airline venture*

- *Disposable income*: and their propensity to spend this disposable income at levels that will sustain the venture in the medium to long term.
- *Answering the questions*: 'Why use you?', 'Why not use you?', 'Why use competitors or opt for an alternative?' and 'Why not use competitors, and why not opt for an alternative?' This is a redefinition of the venturers assessment of their particular strengths and weaknesses. It provides an extremely valuable further point of reference and checking. It is essential that these questions are answered as precisely as possible, rather than resorting to vague or general perceptions.
- *Confidence and security*: the customer and end-user perception that, once a venture is commissioned, it can safely be assumed that it will deliver all the benefits promised or inferred.

As a result of this range of activities a full understanding of the potential of the venture, together with income volumes, can now begin to be drawn up (see box 3.8).

Box 3.8   *The outputs of customer analysis: examples*

Buying a Car

'A few years ago, when my children were young and my job required me to carry a lot of bulky equipment around the country, I looked at a people-carrier vehicle as a potential purchase. They were comfortable, gave good visibility, were reasonably economical, could carry a lot of equipment, were useful for transporting the family, and were configurable so that weekend DIY jobs and shopping excursions could be accomplished quite easily. They were also well made, had received good reports in the motoring press and fell within my budget.

   When the time came to change my car what did I buy? My four-wheeled solution fulfilled very few of my logical needs and I had to personally top up the budget by a few thousand pounds. So much for the needs-based buying behaviour. What I needed and what I wanted were two different agendas.'

This reinforces the point made in Chapter 1 that so much of the investment appraisal process is based on subjectivity, and on identifying the effects of human behaviour on various parts of the whole process. This is a simple example that illustrates just how difficult it is to predict human behaviour; and that this difficulty remains even when the particular subject has worked out more or less logically and rationally what his particular needs are.

Source: Kevin Walker *et al.*, *Creating New Clients*, Cassell, 1998.

The purpose of analysis is to arrive at the conclusion as to whether or not a venture idea is worth pursuing. The result of analysis is a detailed understanding of the whole context in which investment is being considered. This then becomes the basis, in turn, for deciding whether to progress or withdraw from the initiative. Assuming progress is to be made, each party can then establish its own aims and objectives, and its own desired outcomes for the particular venture, in the context in which it is being considered.

AIMS AND OBJECTIVES

Aims and objectives are then drawn up independently by all those involved. They need to be as precise as possible. They should be produced in such a way that they are:

- specific
- measurable
- achievable
- resourced
- time-constrained.

They are then put together by all those involved to see if what is required from the venture is mutually compatible, mutually exclusive, capable or incapable of reconciliation and harmonisation. Using the model above, the central issue is achievability in the context in which the venture is being planned.

It is also necessary, at this stage, to assess the dominance–dependency elements. For example, it may be that a backer will say 'We require you to do this as a condition of our support.' At that point the venturer needs to assess fully what they are now being required to commit to, and whether or not this is feasible. Or it may be that the venturer feels sufficiently confident of their overall ability to attract investment that they impose conditions that cause some potential backers to withdraw.

It is further certain that there will be divergent aims and objectives. These have to be recognised and accommodated at the outset, so that steps can be taken to ensure their effective management during the progress of the venture (this is dealt with in Chapter 8).

Dominant Stakeholders' Aims and Objectives

As stated in Chapter 1, in many situations, dominance of financial interests needs to be understood. For example, it may (and does) occur that mergers and takeovers are pushed through, in spite of the fact that nobody wanted them except the financial interest. When this does happen, the financial interest invariably states that the purpose is to achieve 'synergies' or 'economies of scale'. These phrases are often both telegenic and share-holder-friendly. However, they are very seldom followed up in simple and direct terms explaining exactly what they do mean in the particular context. It is therefore necessary to consider this in detail.

Synergy

Synergy simply means that 'the whole is greater than the some of its parts'. Those who (with integrity) advocate company mergers do so on the basis that the new organisation will outperform the two previously independent companies working alone.

Closely related to this is the phrase 'economies of scale'. This is the phrase used to describe increases in output or productivity, or the reduction of unit costs. In simple terms, these are each of supreme interest to investors and venturers alike, and also to company directors and managers concerned with getting the best from scarce and finite resources. The purpose on the part of those investing in achieving economies of scale is to drive down all costs. Economies of scale may be sought either through improving output in the existing situation, or merging two or more companies and then subsequently lowering the fixed cost base so that the output cost is reduced in comparison to what it was before when the companies operated independently of each other.

In practice, this seldom works (see Preface). The following criticisms have to be recognised.

Shareholders and their representatives　The greatest criticism of synergy and economies of scale is that these are used as part of the process of justifying and then pushing through mergers, acquisitions and takeovers that are in nobody else's interests. These parties gain their returns at the time when the initiative is first agreed in the form of increased share prices, increased commissions on the sale and acquisition of shares. Success or otherwise of the new merged organisation, in terms applicable to everyone else – staff, customers and community – only becomes apparent much later.

Costs　Insufficient attention is invariably paid to the costs incurred in seeking to achieve synergies and economies of scale. These increased costs are:

- Redundancies, in which staff are paid, very often extremely well, to cease working for the organisation (see box 3.9).
- Sale of assets – at first sight, this looks like a marginal benefit. However, once it becomes known that an organisation is keen to dispose of its surplus property and equipment, the price always falls (see box 3.10).
- Harmonisation of terms and conditions of employment – it is still quite usual for those engaging in mergers and takeovers to ignore the costs involved in harmonising terms and conditions of employment and resolving any anomalies (see box 3.11).
- Creating an identity for the new organisation – it is invariably assumed that, because one or both of the independent organisations come into the new situation with a good reputation, this will therefore naturally continue into the future.

- Production and output capacity may become extremely high on paper but not sustainable in terms of sales in the markets served; or not sustainable at the prices desired or demanded. While general synergies and economies of scale give output cost advantages, this still needs to be capable of being fulfilled through sales performance.
- The human aspects of the companies involved may be incompatible. This is usually for reasons of organisation culture clash, management and supervisory style clash, pay and reward anomalies, differences in procedures, reporting relationships, involvement with trade unions, use and application of technology.
- The commercial aspects of the organisations involved may be incompatible; and this includes special reference to production methods, quality assurance, supply-side relations, distribution, customer service, marketing and sales activities.

Any attempt to achieve synergy or economies of scale must account for these. If the decision is then taken to go ahead, these aspects have to be resourced as part of the investment process. The potential effects of each of these aspects needs to be written into the forecast and projection calculations. Further key issues then need to be addressed.

Box 3.9   *Redundancy costs: examples*

- *Barclays plc*: In 1996 the Barclays Banking Group went through a major restructuring programme. There was extensive investment in new premises, technology, staff retraining programmes, and there were redundancies. Voluntary redundancy packages were offered that were so attractive, the redundancy exercise had to be rethought. The purpose stated by the company was to achieve 'economies of scale' and to make the company *more competitive*. In 1998 the company declared the total cost of the venture as being £270 million. Rather than achieving 'economies of scale', it had pushed up its fixed cost base by £270 million – and this would now have to be serviced by seeking economies in operations elsewhere.
- *Local government*: At the opposite end of the scale, local government organisations are encouraged to seek redundancies whenever costs have to be cut. These drives are initiated by councillors and other elected or appointed bodies, and senior managers acquiesce in their delivery. Invariably, redundancies are sought at the frontline of activities. Those most vulnerable to redundancy in local government

are teachers and social workers, and other service providers such as librarians. These staff are normally not paid off at anything like the levels indicated in the Barclays example above. Nevertheless, the result is not to drive down unit or operating costs, but rather to ensure that services become more expensive to deliver, and because there are fewer staff, there is a greater workload imposed on those that remain. The redundancy approach has therefore the summary effect of ensuring that services are reduced in quality, increased in unit cost, and are of less overall value to the end-users and consumers.

Box 3.10 *Disposal of assets*

- *Kent County Council*: In 1997 Kent County Council proposed the relocation of its headquarters and corporate staff away from their base at Springfield to other locations in Maidstone (the county town). At an early stage in the process, the Asda supermarket chain got wind of the move and offered the County Council £11.5 million for the site. This was refused on the grounds that plans had not yet been finalised. Asda consequently looked elsewhere for a super-market site for the town of Maidstone, and the opportunity was lost. In 1999 the site was sold to a property and finance group for £5.5 million.
- *Care in the community*: The stated purpose of the Care in the Community health and social programme was to enable the most vulnerable members of society to live as normal a life as possible. They were to be moved out of institutions and given safe accom-modation in the community, and the institutions in which they had hitherto been housed were to be sold off. This was extremely attractive to those concerned with public health and social service finances, because the shortfalls in budgets could be reduced through the sale of assets. One such asset was the Chartham mental hospital near Canterbury in Kent. At the point at which the 'Care in the Community' initiative was implemented, there was universal support from the health and social service authorities because the site would fetch £23 million. Accordingly, in 1989, the hospital was put on the market at this price. At the beginning of the Year 2000 it remains derelict – and unsold.

Box 3.11   *Children's charity merger*

In 1997 two children's charities operating in the south-west of England merged. Both needed to cut costs and overheads, and the residential property accruing to the new merged organisation would give much greater flexibility in placing 'at risk' children in suitable accommodation.

A social services consultant was hired to address the anomalies in staff terms and conditions of employment. He proposed a twelve-month strategy by which this would be resolved.

He was dismissed from the project after three months. He was replaced by a small local firm of management consultants who proposed very much the same approach over a similar period of time. This firm lasted four months. At the end of this period, the governors of the new merged organisation took the decision to proceed on their own initiative.

The process failed. To address the problems that now became serious issues and grievances, the charity was forced to hire an expensive firm of employment lawyers to handle employment tribunal cases, and to resolve disputes and grievances piecemeal, as and when they arose.

The process was completed in mid-1999. The costs incurred over the two-and-a-half-year period of transition were greater than if the organisations had continued to operate as two separate entities. It also had a knock-on effect on the primary work of the new merged organisation, in that three social services departments no longer referred children in their care and under their supervision to the particular charity.

Policy

Investment policy is concerned with:

- the areas of industry, commerce or public sector to be invested in
- how the work is to be carried out
- how the process is to be managed.

This assessment is necessary in order to understand at the outset when and how money and other resources are to be put up, how much of each is likely to be required at each stage, and what the consequences of this are. It also gives rise to an initial consideration of what particular contingencies, crises and emergencies may arise and how these might best be handled.

Matching Opportunities and Ventures with Resources

This can usefully be represented as in Figure 3.10.

At first site this appears superficial and obvious. However, the information gathered needs consideration from this point of view, and then reconciling with the aims and objectives of the different parties involved. Above all, it is a further vehicle by which the likelihood of sustaining and

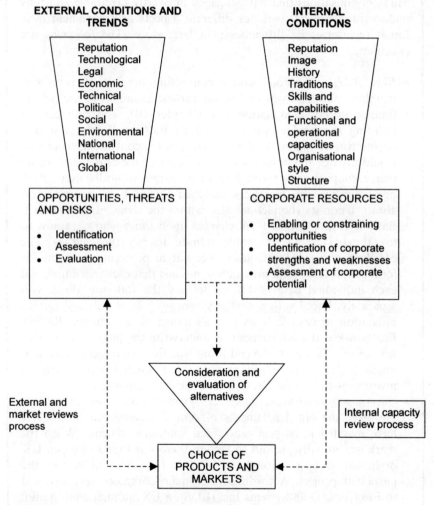

Figure 3.10 *Matching opportunities and ventures with resources*

developing activities in the medium-to-long-term can be assessed. Further issues that require consideration may also become apparent as the result of carrying out this exercise (see box 3.12).

Box 3.12   *Matching opportunities with resources: a note on public sector investment*

This is especially important when engaging in public sector work. Many organisations that have engaged in overtly profitable and fully underwritten project work for different aspects of government have found themselves in difficulties at a later stage. The following are examples.

- *Skye Bridge*: The road bridge connecting the Isle of Skye with mainland Scotland was one of the earliest examples of the private finance initiative in action (see Chapter 10). The contract for building the bridge was awarded to Balfour Beatty, the civil engineering company. Under the terms of the contract the company would provide the finance for the building of the bridge and would then recoup its costs through making charges to bridge users. Both opportunities and resources matched up, and the project went ahead. Upon its completion, also within the terms of the contract, Balfour Beatty imposed toll charges upon those who were now to use the bridge. Local people refused to pay the charges. The company was faced with no choice but to prosecute. Lawyers for local people faced with prosecution insisted that each individual, and each individual case of refusal to pay the toll, was dealt with separately. Faced with potentially enormous legal bills and serious disruption to cash flow as well as return on investment, Balfour Beatty asked the government to underwrite the project costs. This was agreed. However, the end result was that the project came in at much higher cost to government, and much lower return on investment to Balfour Beatty, than had been envisaged.
- *Government department computer systems*: From the early 1990s onwards, the big departments of central government in the UK have invested heavily in centralised computer systems. When the work was initially put out to tender, there was found to be no UK organisation large enough to be able to deliver or service the particular project. Accordingly, the main contracts were awarded to Electronic Data Systems Inc. (EDS), a US multinational. Again, on the face of it, both opportunities and resources existed to the

satisfaction of all concerned. However, when the systems were introduced, problems quickly became apparent. Government officials had found themselves unable to explain adequately what it was exactly that they wanted, or what the outputs of the particular systems were supposed to be. EDS, on the other hand, were used to delivering large and complex systems for both public and commercial bodies in the USA, but had failed to understand the overall culture and ways of working in UK central government bodies. Moreover, staff training, maintenance and after-sales arrangements, and provisions for system upgrades, were not written into the original contracts. Again, the results have been that the services provided have been delivered less efficiently and effectively than previously, and have come to cost far more than anticipated.

The main lessons from each of these examples is that the outcomes could have been predicted as a range of possibilities if the investment strategy process had been worked through, or if the matching opportunities with resources approach had been considered from a broad perspective. As a consequence of not doing this properly, the particular aspects of government have found themselves overpaying for something that was supposed to reduce costs and charges; while the venturers involved have lost reputation, as well as having expertise and technology that could have been better used elsewhere, tied up in these ventures.

Levels of Investment

It is essential to have a clear idea of:

- the total levels of investment required, sought and offered, and whether there are any differences apparent; and if so, whether there are consequences for the viability of the venture;
- the different levels that are required at the various stages of the work as stated above;
- whether investment is to be consequent upon the successful outcome of the different steps in the process, and the likely and possible consequences of this;
- any possible variations in demand for finance as the result of unforeseen or unlikely circumstances or occurrences.

This needs consideration from the point of view of upward variation (i.e. where investment outperforms expectations) and the circumstances under which this might occur; and also downward variation (i.e. where targets are not met).

CONCLUSIONS

This form of approach to investment has the purpose of ensuring that everyone involved knows what they are going into, how they are going into it, and why. It is also usefully carried out even when a particular initiative is being driven by narrow and overwhelming shareholder, stockbroker or finance interests. This is because those who have to manage the particular organisation or situation in the future can at least gauge the likely scale of problems and identify those matters which the narrow interest failed to recognise (or else recognised but chose to ignore).

It should also be clear by now that investment strategy is a process. It is concerned with building solid foundations on which effective and mutually profitable ventures take place, and ensuring that the situation that emerges is managed from inception to completion.

Above all, it ensures that fundamental questions of compatibility of purpose, aims and objectives are apparent at the outset. Any problems or issues in the areas of confidence, expectations and overall acceptability also start to emerge at this stage, and these must now be addressed.

4 Behavioural Aspects of the Investment Process

INTRODUCTION

Small, private and individual investors in the UK are most likely to put their money into bank and building society deposit accounts. This is in spite of the fact that, over anything but the shortest periods of time, they give substantially lower rates of return than personal equity plans (PEPs), tax-exempt special savings schemes (TESSAs) and individual savings accounts (ISAs), share portfolios and unit trusts. The reason for this is simple: it is because they perceive that they know, understand and trust these institutions to look after their money (see box 4.1).

Similarly, independent financial advisers and financial service companies know that they will only persuade individuals to invest with them once they have built up a perceived personal relationship, understanding and confidence, in addition to being able to satisfy the prospective client of their professional acumen and integrity.

This also holds true for major corporate investments in commercial, public and global ventures and projects. Ultimately, no effective corporate investment decision is taken purely on the basis of mutual, professional and operational compatibility: personal confidence is essential also (see box 4.2). The thrust of this chapter is to tackle this critical aspect of the investment process.

CONFIDENCE

The first step is establishing confidence. The outcome of this is that:

- People buy if they buy you.
- People buy if you can fulfil and satisfy their needs and wants.
- People buy if you can lead them to the conclusion that they have needs which must be addressed and that they are really looking for a solution to these newly discovered (and now apparently mountainous) needs.
- People buy for two reasons – because they need something or because it makes them feel good.
- People buy (or choose not to buy) as the result of the real or perceived relationship that exists; and if no satisfactory relationship is deemed to

69

exist then people never have complete confidence in the venture or proposal.

Confidence is therefore initially built on understanding and accepting that everyone has personal needs and wants, even from a corporate or professional situation. This is only possible if some form of personal harmony is generated. The effective management of investment initiatives therefore concentrates equally on managing the process and managing those involved.

Box 4.1   *Perception and investment: examples from the banking sector*

Just how strong these perceptions are may be illustrated by two examples from the banking sector.

- *Bank of Credit and Commerce International*: The Bank of Credit and Commerce International (BCCI) was founded in 1973 by Aga Hasan Abedi. The bank was founded on strong and overriding principles of totality of service and complete integrity. 'The Bank of Credit and Commerce International exists because people throughout the world and through the centuries have changed their status and place of residence. One wave of immigration and of emigration has followed another. In the wake of these movements follow transfers of capital and commodities, and BCCI has made it its business to ease that flow through the supply of credit and banking services' (Aga Hasan Abedi, 1985). The bank found strong identity with immigrant communities from the Indian subcontinent in the UK, and by 1997 had built up a basis of 130,000 personal accounts. The distinctive cultural base, and high degree of perceived familiarity, caused those opening personal accounts at a bank to believe that they had at last found someone who would genuinely look after their personal financial interests. The bank collapsed in 1990, and the founders, including Abedi, were indicted for fraud, the laundering of drug money, and the theft of savings from people's personal accounts.
- *Barings*: Barings Bank was founded in 1789, and initially made its money investing in trading ventures between the UK, Holland and the Far East. In recent years, as a merchant bank, it diversified into investing in, and underwriting, commodity trading and exchanges, and dealings in foreign currencies and stocks and shares. It had a long-established name, and was well regarded by important people. Because of its lineage and impressive past history, the company

enjoyed a queue of organisations and companies seeking to attract venture and investment finance from the bank. The bank collapsed because a single foreign exchange and futures dealer, Nick Leeson, was able to run up debts totalling £800 million while the company's senior management remained in total ignorance of what he was doing. Called to account for this, the senior management line was that Leeson was known, he was trusted, and that he appeared to know what he was doing. For the two-year period preceding the bank's collapse in 1992, Leeson had received no formal supervision or appraisal of the performance of his ventures.

Source: R. S. Lessem, *The Global Business*, Prentice Hall International, 1987; Sarah Hall, 'Nick Leeson: Rogue Trader', Macmillan, 1996.

Box 4.2 *'Better the devil you know'*

The above phrase reinforces the point that it is much easier to attract investment from known and familiar sources of finance and resources, than to gain it from new providers. 'Better the devil you know' indeed refers to the person not the product or service.

Effective investment is dependent upon:

- being a known and therefore trustworthy provider;
- knowing the less tangible appeals which will persuade individuals working on behalf of their organisation's interests to support the proposal;
- 'you will never make a serious error in judgement if you expect your prospects and clients to make decisions on personal rather than organisational consequences'.

None of these points ever appears on invitations to tender or invitations to invest. They are nevertheless key behavioural factors in the securing of investment for ventures; or conversely, looking for projects in which to invest.

Source: R. Carlson, *Personal Selling Strategies for Consultants and Professionals*, Cassell, 1994.

MUTUALITY OF INTEREST

With confidence comes the willingness to open up; and this, in turn, leads to establishing an initial mutuality of interest. This takes the following forms.

- Mutual personal interest, preference and liking; or disinterest, antagonism and dislike.
- Mutual professional interest; or conflict.
- Mutual interest in the proposal; or disinterest.
- Mutual openness and honesty concerning the proposal; or dishonesty and duplicity.
- Mutual willingness to raise issues; or mutual unwillingness to raise issues or tendency to ignore them.
- Mutual understanding of the other's position; or perceived and tainted understanding of the other's position.
- Mutual respect and trust; or mutual disrespect and mistrust.

This is based on personal confidence as well as perceived professional capability (see box 4.3).

Box 4.3 *Real Madrid*

In the football industry, Real Madrid is one of the most prestigious names in the world. Over the years, the club has invested heavily in bringing the best and most glamorous players on to its books; and has also invested heavily in stadium, training and educational facilities to ensure that it preserves its position.

During the period of the 1990s, however, the questions of personal confidence, as well as perceived professional capability, have come under increasing strain. The overall result of this is to damage the results of the club, and to draw attention to the consequent reductions of the value of investment in players (in which many players are now perceived to have been vastly overpaid for, especially when they are sold on at extremely reduced prices). This has also called into question the integrity and capability of the management and training staff. Since 1990 the club has had seven different coaches; and one, Jupp Heynckes, was dismissed the day after the club had won the European Champions Cup because it was felt by the club ownership that the overall performance over the season had not been good enough (the club finished fifth in the league).

Because of the high-profile nature of the industry in Spain, the media have been quick to draw attention to the increasing level of the club's debt; real and perceived lack of motivation and performance on the part of some of the players; and any shortcomings in results or performance.

As a result, some star players have chosen to accept the extremely high level of wages on offer for a period of a fixed-term contract, and then to move on, greatly enriched, but without necessarily having delivered the commensurate performance.

The overall effect has therefore been to reduce the total value of the investment and to increase the level of debt needing to be served. It has also led to the need for managers and coaches to generate confidence through the quest for real and perceived high-value and high-quality performers. Those players falling under this category, once they have realised the totality of the situation, have therefore been able to command increased salaries and fees, which, in turn, is continuing to compound the problem at the end of the twentieth century.

MOTIVATION

Ideally, the motivation to be involved in the proposal and to see it through to a successful conclusion should be mutual. It is important to consider the possibility that it may not be so. For example, one party may be having its arm heavily twisted to become involved in the first place, and may only do so very much against its better judgement.

In other cases, a party may be under great pressure to gain the investment or to make the investment as a condition of their own individual career progression or to earn commission or bonuses. This was the basis on which a great deal of personal investment and pension selling fell into disrepute in the UK from the mid-1980s onwards. This has been further exacerbated by the fact that nobody who was sold an inappropriate, unsuitable or under-performing personal investment plan or personal pension scheme has ever been prosecuted.

Expectancy

A useful and well-researched theoretical way of looking at the question of motivation in investment situations is to establish the relationship between expectation, effort and rewards (see Figure 4.1).

Applying this to investment situations and initiatives, we arrive at the model shown in Figure 4.2. This constitutes the relationship between what is expected, the rewards and returns that are to accrue, and the commitment

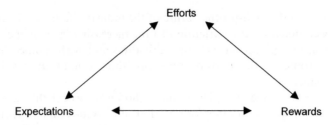

Figure 4.1   *Expectancy model*

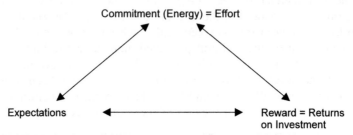

Figure 4.2   *Expectancy model translated into investment appraisal criteria*

(including invariably the effort and energy) necessary to ensure that the rewards are achieved and expectations are met (see Figures 4.3 and 4.4).

Seen from this point of view, confidence in the venture is maintained as long as the three elements are kept in balance. Problems arise when one or more becomes unbalanced. If rewards are not forthcoming as the result of efforts and energy expended, or if the effort and energy expended has to be increased in order to secure the original level of reward, this especially always causes loss of confidence.

From this, certain precise guidelines can be established.

- If specific percentage per annum returns are required, investment must be made where these are forthcoming.
- If returns are required in six months, then investments must be in areas where these are achievable.
- If investment in a certain sector or project is required, then the returns offered by that sector or project must be understood and acceptable – and accepted.
- If any of these factors change, investors must be prepared to change with them.

There are also factors less overtly financial to be considered. These nevertheless affect the effectiveness of investment, and especially the relationship between expectation and rewards.

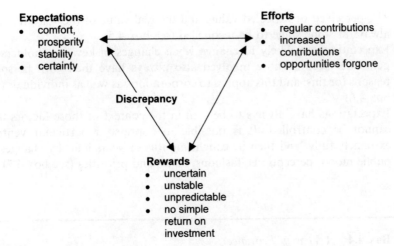

Figure 4.3   *Example: the expectancy model applied to personal pension investment*

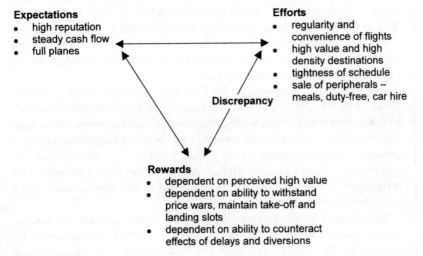

Figure 4.4   *Example: the expectancy model applied to investment in a low cost airline venture*

- If a particular reputation or image is required, then investments must be made in areas where this is possible (see box 4.4).
- If synergies or economies of scale are required, then attention has to be paid to those areas of the investment that will produce them.
- If there is a political drive for the venture, then the consequences of this have to be addressed.

- The perceived or expected value, and the real value of the venture, have always at some stage to be reconciled (see box 4.5).
- Expectations are likely to change when changes in key stakeholders or personnel occur. Those involved also always have their own personal reasons for this; and this applies to corporations as well as individuals (see box 4.6).
- Expectations have always to be seen in the context of those factors that cannot be controlled. It is possible to appraise a particular venture extremely fully, and then be caught months or years later by changes in public mood, perceptions, fashions, tastes and priorities (see box 4.7).

Box 4.4   *A Year in Provence*

A Year in Provence was written by Peter Mayle, an advertising executive, about his life and experiences when he relocated with his wife to the Provence region of the south of France. It was published in 1986 and became a major bestseller, selling more than one million copies. Companies queued up to invest in ventures that would turn the book into a film or television series.

The film rights were sold to the BBC who turned it into a television series. John Thaw and Lindsey Duncan, at the time the country's leading actor and actress, were chosen to play the key roles. Other high profile actors and actresses sought, and were awarded, cameo roles during the different parts of the series. Satisfied that they had all the components of a sure-fire winner in place, the BBC produced and transmitted the series in six parts, confident of world-wide sales and a massive returns on investment.

The venture failed. Ratings dropped by 40 per cent after transmission of the first episode. Viewing figures for the first episode were 14.7 million; by the time of the sixth and last episode, those figures were down to 5.4 million. The series could not be sold abroad at any price, let alone the original levels envisaged.

The failure of the project, and the losses incurred, were ascribed by internal reviewers at the BBC to being 'one of those things'. The other key players in the venture, however, were much more concerned to address the broader perspective. In particular, Peter Mayle, John Thaw and Lindsey Duncan quickly engaged themselves in other projects to limit the damage caused to their reputations as the result of the series not meeting expectations.

Box 4.5 *Perceived and actual values*

- *The Millennium Dome* (2): The Millennium Dome had a perceived value when it was announced of providing a monument to two thousand years of Christianity in the UK. It had a real value only of providing fifteen minutes of fame to the politicians involved. In 1999, if they are speaking off the record, it is virtually impossible to find any politician who is prepared to concede that the project was a good or well-thought-out venture.
- *Eurotunnel* (2): When the proposal for the Channel Tunnel project was drawn up, Eurotunnel produced a short video presentation demonstrating how it would be able to run six passenger shuttles and four freight shuttles per hour. This was used as one of the bases on which future projected levels of income would be achieved. In practice, the company has been able to operate a maximum of four passenger shuttles per hour, and three freight shuttles per hour when operating at full capacity. On the face of it, this appears 'not too bad', and this is one of the phrases used by the company's public relations department to support the present levels of operation. However, in order to achieve the projected levels of service and operation, passenger shuttles need to be increased by 50 per cent and freight shuttles by 33 per cent. These are substantial margins of difference between expected and actual performance and value.

Source: *Daily Telegraph*, 6 September 1999; Eurotunnel, *Strategy for the Use of the Channel Tunnel* (1986).

Box 4.6 *Coal privatisation in the UK*

In 1986 the decision was taken to privatise the National Coal Board, the government-owned company responsible for extracting and delivering coal from mines in the UK. The company name was changed to British Coal, and other organisations were invited to tender for the purchase of the company.

The expectations of the parties involved were as follows.

- The government expected to be able to divest itself of any responsibility for an historically troublesome and controversial industry.

- Kleinwort Benson, the merchant bankers appointed to structure the proposal and conduct the sale, expected to be paid (and subsequently received) huge fees for their part in the process. These fees were delivered at the point of sale, and before any residual effects could be assessed.
- The trade unions expected massive job losses and downturns in terms and conditions of employment.
- Trade unions feared for large downturns in pension contributions on which depended the future viability of the pension funds that had accrued under the years of government management and control, and which were required to service their obligations to ex-miners. It was agreed by government that these obligations would be underwritten.
- RJB Mining plc, the eventual purchasers, were able to buy British Coal eventually for £1, on condition that they met all outstanding liabilities, orders and work in progress. The company further expected to be able to take the substantial mining expertise, property assets and modern mining technology, and develop it and use it for its other activities.

The original range of expectations was simply that British Coal would produce a major contribution to the energy needs of UK industry, and consumer and public services. All these expectations changed, with the consequences indicated above, when the new players were brought into the situation.

Box 4.7   *The effect of future changes: examples*

- *Trident*: The Trident nuclear submarine was developed in the USA during the 1960s and 1970s. In 1975 the UK agreed to purchase 16 Trident submarines from the USA. These would be delivered over the period 1979–95. Their purpose was to maintain and improve the nuclear arsenal capacity of the UK, and to make a broader contribution to the defence of the West, in the face of the threat of war from the USSR. In 1986 it became apparent that the USSR could not sustain itself and would break up; and in 1989 it was pronounced bankrupt. The communist government fell. Countries held by enforced treaty with the USSR (the Warsaw Pact) unilat-

erally looked to the West for inward investment and commercialisation. Trident submarines nevertheless continued to be delivered until
1993, in spite of the fact that they were now obsolete.

- *Manchester United*: In the UK football industry, Manchester United
is one of the most glamorous, prestigious and high-profile names.
However, over the period 1967–92, the club consistently under-
performed. The first step towards addressing this was taken in
1988 with the creation of the club's own football academy. It was
a major investment, the results of which would not be seen for
several years. Performance began to improve. Funds for further
investment and expansion were generated through the sale of shares
on the stock market. The club continued to seek and attract
sponsorship, media coverage and private television rights over the
period. The club also exploited its merchandising potential by selling
replica football strips and other items of perceived value to the
supporters. In 1992 the club won its first championship for 26 years.
Built on a secure financial base, and with a steady stream of young
home-grown players, as well as the ability to attract and retain top
stars from elsewhere, the club became swept along by the globalisa-
tion of top-level football.

The major consequence of this was that supporters' expectations
changed. In terms of performance, the club was now expected to
win everything that it entered. There also remains a feeling among
supporters, however, that, as the club has become so successful, and as
it has continued to raise its charges both for admission to games and
also for merchandise, they are being taken advantage of unfairly by an
institution which perceives itself to be big enough to make its own
rules.

PERCEPTION

Understanding perception, the process of receiving and interpreting information from the external world, is of critical importance in investment
appraisal. This is because the information available and used is:

- often specialist, technical or expert;
- often stated, and sometimes tainted, by its presentation, especially if there
is a strong vested interest present, or if it has been delivered by an expert
working in isolation from a proposed venture. It is therefore easy to
influence the presentation to give the desired effect (see box 4.8).

Box 4.8   *Dealing with perceptions and preconceptions: examples*

- *Financial services*: The financial services industry is required by law
  to include a certain phrase when dealing with prospective investment
  clients. The phrase is: 'Past performance is not a guarantee of future
  performance. The value of investments can go down as well as up.'
  This is at least a first step along the route to ensuring that people do
  not believe in any financial projections for the future as a matter of
  . absolute fact.
- *Public inquiries*: The role and function of public inquiries is to ensure
  that, when major public and commercial investments are made,
  everybody who wishes to do so can put forward their point of view
  and have any questions or burning issues answered. A major side-
  effect of public inquiries is also to ensure that genuine problems and
  limitations of the venture are brought out into the open. A further
  side-effect is to ensure that at least a measure of professional
  understanding is brought to projects that may have been swept into
  life through personal or professional enthusiasm, vested interest or
  political expediency.

Major Aspects of Perception

The major aspects of perception are as follows.

- *Individual and collective perception*: Perception is affected by the individual's own experiences and knowledge of the world. It is also affected by
  socialisation – the interaction between individuals and the different parts
  of society in which they come into contact.
- *Halo effects*: Strong positive or negative characteristics (often visual or
  tactile) are either apparent or inferred, and the rest of the person's
  capabilities and personality traits are assumed from this.
- *First impressions*: The first impression is the instant positioning of someone or something on the individual's perceptual map.
- *Perceptual mapping*: Individuals and groups 'map' everything and everyone with which they come into contact against their past history and
  experiences.
- *Stereotyping*: Stereotyping occurs when a set of characteristics are
  assumed in particular categories of people; and particular categories of
  people are assumed to have that set of characteristics.
- *Self-fulfilling prophecy*: Self-fulfilling prophecy occurs where a prejudgement is ascribed to a particular set of circumstances, and then the

subsequent development of the venture or relationship is measured (and sometimes positively managed) towards this prejudgement.

- *Implicit personality theory*: Implicit personality theory is the process by which people assume that particular characteristics go together – characteristics such as kindness and gentleness; or violence and dishonesty. Personal and professional confidence is called into question: for example, when it becomes apparent that someone with whom you are dealing is both kind and dishonest, or very capable in one area but not in others.
- *Mythology*: Mythology is the process by which people put a largely spurious rationale on the ways in which they organise their information. Common phrases used are: 'in my opinion', 'in my experience', 'in my day, we used to . . .', and these phrases are used to try and gain some dominance over a situation in which people have very little genuine experience or expertise.
- *Adaptation*: Adaptation is the definition of perception as a continuous process. People's view of the world is constantly being influenced and changed by circumstances and surroundings, pressures and priorities, and the source of those pressures and priorities.
- *Comfort zones*: Comfort zones are the physical, behavioural and psychological areas in which the individuals or groups are comfortable and familiar. Comfort and familiarity are arrived at as a result of habit, success, liking and understanding.
- *Editing*: Editing occurs when people form a particular view of the world with which they are comfortable. They then edit out those parts that contrast with their comfortable view of the world.
- *Closure*: Closure occurs when people see part of a particular picture or situation, and then *complete* the unknown or unseen parts to form a whole, again normally one with which they are familiar and comfortable.

In investment appraisal, it is especially important to be aware of the following.

- *Halo effects*: A high reputation, or presentation by a well-known (sometimes public) figure or corporation, does not necessarily mean that the venture will come to fruition.
- *Comfort zone*: A high reputation, or being advocated by a well-known figure or corporation, makes it very easy to jump to the conclusion that it *is* right and that it *will* succeed.

Editing and Closure

When the information available is both specialist and limited, people tend to latch on to those bits that they do understand. This becomes their first impression, and this, in turn, causes a strong and initially favourable or unfavourable disposition. This can be very hard to shake. It also becomes the basis for further discussion and appraisal, whether or not a basic complete grasp of the issue has in fact been achieved.

The process of editing also occurs when people ignore – edit out – those things that they do not wish to see. This is a form of denial of one or more aspects of the venture or process. For example, those who invest in pharmaceuticals and chemicals edit out or deny animal experimentation and vivisection; those who invest in defence projects deny that the weaponry is to be used for offensive and oppressive actions, as well as defence.

A part of editing also refers to things that are not carried out because people do not understand them. This is usually because they do not have direct access to the required expertise, nor the patience to acquire it for themselves. It may also occur, most insidiously, when the expert comes up with (for whatever reason) the *wrong* answers – or when they come up with the right answer, but for some reason, this has become unacceptable to those who commission them to do the work. Rather than accepting this, those involved seek other sources of expertise that will come up with the required answers (see box 4.9).

Box 4.9 *Industrial and commercial ventures in British Columbia*

For the past 150 years, logging has been a major industry in the Canadian province of British Columbia, on the west coast of Canada. In the 1980s, following a rapid increase in activities and the consequent depletion of tree stocks, and also because of environmental concerns, the British Columbia Provincial Government commissioned Michael Porter, the business policy and strategy expert, to look at alternative sources of employment for the province, and to make proposals for the design and development of commercial ventures that could be used to support this.

Porter conducted extensive research across the province, and also consulted with the central Canadian government in Ottawa. He produced a set of recommendations that proposed the development of an enhanced and improved transport infrastructure, and the development of tourist resorts both for the west coast of mainland Canada and also for the western and northern coasts of Vancouver Island. He paid specific attention to the environmental consequences, and to implications for the design of the developments that were undertaken.

The proposals were debated at length, both in the provincial government of British Columbia, and also within committees of the central government. Eventually the proposals were rejected.

> In the late 1990s the provincial government of British Columbia produced its own proposals for the replacement of the logging industry. These would be based on tourism and included – the development of a transport infrastructure, and the commercialisation of resorts on the west coast of mainland Canada, and on the northern and western coasts of Vancouver Island!!
>
> The consensus has clearly been arrived at that Porter's proposals were right. The problem was that he was the wrong person to deliver them.

CULTURAL ASPECTS

Culture may simply be defined as 'the ways in which things are done here'; or more thoroughly as 'the summation of attitudes, behaviour, values and beliefs' in a particular sector of society.

Culture is shaped and developed by age, history, traditions, myths and legends; and also by the historic and prevailing religious and social priorities. It is influenced by economic activity and the real and perceived value, prosperity and quality of life that this brings.

Culture varies from place to place, between and within organisations, projects and ventures. The key here, in investment appraisal terms, is acceptability – that what is being proposed is acceptable in the cultural and behavioural context in which it is to take place. In every investment appraisal, the following should always be assessed.

- Something that is rationally or economically right may not work if, for any reason, it is culturally unacceptable.
- Something that is rationally or economically wrong may be made to work if the cultural or social drives are nevertheless overwhelming.
- If something is culturally unacceptable it will not work however strong the economic case.
- If something is morally reprehensible or revolting, it may nevertheless be made to work if sufficiently strong cultural drives are engaged (see box 4.10).

This part of investment appraisal is normally either neglected altogether, or else not fully thought through. In particular, the ability of human behaviour to limit or deny success to overtly highly desirable and assuredly profitable investments cannot be overstated. However good, profitable or effective an idea may overtly be, it will not work if people do not want it to, or do not want it.

Box 4.10   *The cultural aspects of investment: examples*

Examples of the cultural aspects of investment appraisal are as follows.

- *Body Shop*: By paying attention to the cultural, social and ethical aspects of both investment and consumer behaviour, the Body Shop was able to develop its organic cosmetics business from nothing into a £500-million-per-annum turnover. The business commenced trading in 1975, and its development took place at a time when those consumers with spending power had ever greater choice; and those consumers with less spending power were having to make increasingly 'rational' choices about their purchases.
- *United Nations*: From the 1970s onwards, the United Nations has sought to promote birth control and population management programmes in South America, Africa and Asia. One such programme consisted of issuing free birth control pills to women of childbearing age in parts of India. The programme was initiated in response to pressures both from the Indian government and also from fledgling women's groups in the country. The programme was a failure. While it was true that Indian women – rationally – did not want to keep bearing children, the social and cultural pressures upon them nevertheless required that they continue to do so. In some cases, the women involved took the birth pills and made them into necklaces. This satisfied the requirements of the UN programme that the pills were indeed being used; and the local social pressures that nothing was being done to limit the childbearing.
- *Windscale*: The Windscale nuclear reprocessing plant in north-western England was opened in 1969. From its very early stages of operation it was dogged by pollution scandals. It was 'repositioned' in 1980. Attention was drawn to the amount of work and therefore prosperity that it brought into the region; its name was changed to Sellafield; and this was reinforced by a policy of perceived openness, supported by a massive and high-quality public relations campaign. As the result of this, it has been able to greatly expand its sphere of operations and draw in nuclear fuel reprocessing work from all over the world.
- *Speer*: The Speer civil and mechanical engineering company was accorded the status of favoured contractor when the Nazis came to power in Germany in the 1930s. Because of this, it was awarded many prestigious and valuable building and construction contracts by the regime. In 1938 it was first invited to tender for the building of concentration camps; and a year later submitted proposals, again in

> response to invitation, for death camps and extermination machinery. Because it was institutionalised by the instruments of state, and because of the overwhelmingly powerful culture of racial supremacy and purity, the company was able to attract civil and mechanical engineering graduates from the finest universities in Germany to produce the specifications for this work.

POWER AND INFLUENCE

It is usual to define the following sources of power and influence.

- *Charismatic*: which refers to a special aspect of a leader's personality, or that of another dominant personality.
- *Traditional*: this refers to kinship or favouritism as a basis for allocating power. Thus, for example, son follows father in inheritance; or high-paying or prestigious jobs are awarded to favourites.
- *Legal-rational*: where power and influence are regulated by rules and norms and legitimised by law and custom.
- *Reward power*: in which persons with authority over others have the ability to give or withhold rewards (both financial and non-financial).
- *Physical power*: this is the capability to get somebody to do something through the use or threat of physical force.
- *Expert power*: in which knowledge and expertise give power and the ability to influence courses of action.
- *Referent power*: this is power based on personal friendships and relationships of superiors and subordinates.
- *Legitimate power*: if subordinates believe that they are subordinate, then they legitimise the power of their superior.
- *Hierarchical power*: in which power, authority and influence are accorded as the result of rank, status or job title held.
- *The power of norms and customs*: the ability to set standards, and enforce patterns of behaviour, that enable the ways in which people will act to be predicted with a degree of certainty.

It is essential that this is understood when assessing the specific drives behind particular ventures. Of especial importance are the following.

- *Legal-rational*: Investments may be driven by people who have sufficient authority to take a decision without wider reference. This is positive so long as those in such positions have expertise as well as influence. At the opposite end of the scale is the ability to ride roughshod over expert advice, or to ignore it altogether.

- *Expert*: Investments may be driven by people who have sufficient expertise in their own area to understand what the prognoses are for particular initiatives. This becomes corrupted when expertise is used as the basis for pursuing other ends such as generating personal projects or making a personal reputation. This also occurs through the process of blocking ventures that are known and understood to be worthwhile, again using expertise as the basis for doing this; and this is normally done for personal reasons, or in matters of organisational realpolitik.
- *Personality and charisma*: This needs to be understood where ventures are undertaken because they have been energised by somebody through the sheer force of their personality. This is positive so long as personality is informed by expertise. It is both damaging and destructive when it is not. It is a particular problem when dealing with powerful and influential politicians, and shareholders' representatives.
- *Blocking*: The power to block is endemic in all aspects of organisational behaviour and business life. In the specific area of investment appraisal, it occurs when expertise and authority are used to deny initiatives (as above). It also occurs when any party to the venture loses confidence or changes agenda, and yet does not have the full confidence of their position upheld by the others involved. They therefore tend to use their expertise or authority to slow down progress, and dilute the venture, in the hope that others will take the hint. Again, this is not conducive to effective investment activities.

LEADERSHIP

Every investment decision requires direction, responsibility, measurement, evaluation, energy and steering. This applies equally whether it is an individual's bank or building society deposit account, or a major and complex public project. In the former case, responsibility for investment performance is ultimately accepted by the depositor, who has the function of evaluating the performance of the deposit, and of moving the funds elsewhere if it is not satisfactory.

In more complex cases, it is usual for someone to take charge of each stage of the venture. Thus leadership in investment projects is a process; and this brings with it its own problems. For example, someone may be unwilling to hand over the reins when their particular responsibility for direction of the venture has ended. Or the person in charge at a particular stage may nevertheless be manipulated by others with greater personality or perceived authority. Others may pull rank, organisational or political influence in order to get the person in charge at a particular stage to do things their way.

This is a major problem when those at the core of the venture know that they are being driven by a powerful stakeholder or vested interest, especially where there are large short-term gains to be made, or where there is an overwhelming political drive.

It is therefore necessary to have someone in overall charge, agreeable and acceptable to all parties to the venture, to ensure that problems in the process of leadership are kept to a minimum.

Anyone in this position has therefore to be able to understand this, and to take responsibility for reconciling the divergent interests in any venture or proposal. Those committed to the venture must therefore be able to recognise the process elements, recognise the particular problems and issues that are likely to arise; and from this, agree to appoint a single figure who will take responsibility for the overall inception and direction of the venture (see box 4.11).

Box 4.11 *Leadership and investment: Alistair Morton*

In 1986 Eurotunnel was awarded the contract to build and operate the Channel Tunnel. The company was formed of a consortium of five UK and five French construction companies.

Initially, the venture had two Chief Executives – Alistair Morton and Jacques Genard. This, it was felt, would reconcile the cultural difficulties that might become a problem if one or the other was appointed to direct the whole project.

It very quickly became apparent that this would not work. There was a perception that each of the key figures would be looking after their national vested interest, rather than serving the priorities of the project. Accordingly, Genard was appointed President of the venture, with special remit to deal with shareholders and financial interests, while Morton was appointed sole Chief Executive, responsible for awarding the contract, and then managing the construction and completion of the project.

Because leadership and authority were now clearly defined, the cultural problems failed to materialise. Both ways of working and also management style were designed so as to transcend these matters – anyone attending any site or company meeting at any time had to be prepared that this meeting would be conducted in either English or French. Full flexibility of working was ensured on both sides of the project itself, and the highest common factors were always applied when designing site practice, safety measures, delivery of materials and quality of workmanship.

The company subsequently ran into serious financial difficulties; and one of the reasons why these were able to be resolved, at least to the extent of keeping the project open, was because the finance industry had a known and understood point of contact in whom they ultimately had confidence.

CONCLUSIONS

The purpose of looking at investment appraisal from these different points of view is to ensure that the human and other non-quantifiable aspects of ventures and proposals are fully assessed. This is to ensure that, as well as satisfying the financial projections and calculations, attention is paid to the wants and desires, as well as the needs, of all those involved.

To be effective, proposals have therefore to be:

- *understandable*: as fully as possible from the point of view of all those involved; and also all of those who are to be affected by the carrying out and completion of the venture;
- *acceptable*: to all those involved, including reference to both overall projections and also individual aims and objectives;
- *presentable or marketable*: they must be capable of being designed and delivered in ways that both those involved, and also those affected, can identify with, and be comfortable with, once commitment to purpose has been achieved.

Only when this is understood alongside the financial projections, can effective investment decisions be taken.

5 Decision-Making Processes

INTRODUCTION

The purpose of this chapter is to bring together all of the material covered in the previous three chapters as the basis for taking effective investment decisions.

It is usual to identify basic decision-making processes along the following lines.

AN ARCHETYPE OF DECISION-MAKING

Decision-making normally has the following elements.

- *Problem definition*: This may appear obvious, but the effects and consequences of a particular course of action will not be fully understood if the issue in question is not accurately and fully defined at the outset; and if this definition is not agreed by all concerned.
- *Process determination*: Much of this depends on the cultural and other behavioural pressures on the particular venture. This ensures that questions concerning credibility, authority, acceptability, priority and ways of working are addressed at the outset.
- *Timescale*: If decisions are required in limited timescales, there is a trade-off between information, evaluation and cost. The longer a decision can be left, the better the chances of gaining full or adequate information. On the other hand, if a quick decision is required, it becomes riskier, because alternative courses of action may have to be evaluated to a level of incompleteness.
- *Information gathering*: The better the information on which it is based, the more effective the decision is likely to be. On the other hand, very few decisions can be made with perfect information; and this problem is exacerbated when time constraints are involved, or else when there is a prohibitive cost in gathering the information. The quality of the information gathered is also important, as is the quality of its evaluation.
- *Alternatives*: In any investment situation, there are always at least two alternatives – to progress or not. At this stage, the consequences of following and not following proposed courses of action will be evaluated. It is also necessary to fully evaluate all of the possible positive steps that may have become apparent as the result of determining the process and gathering information. Other factors now start to present themselves with

89

a fair degree of accuracy – including costings, profits, returns on investment, costs and benefits.

- *Implementation*: This is the point of action; and it is arrived at as the result of working through the previous stages of the process. Decisions always, in turn, affect others, and the consequences of this need also to be fully evaluated. Proposed courses of action also have effects on others and these should be prepared for this, particularly if there is any adverse element in the decision, or if resources are being clawed away from other activities in order to ensure that the particular venture is a success. The process is not an end in itself. It always leads to other courses of action, and opportunities and prospects.

- *Review*: Once a decision is taken, review and evaluation processes must be established to ensure that progress is kept under constant surveillance, and that any problems that may be inherent are noted and dealt with in good time. This also becomes the basis of evaluating the action in question for measures of success, failure, cost, profit, return on investment, loss, effects and consequences.

It is a simple process that, if understood and followed as fully as possible, minimises the risks and uncertainties of the particular venture; and also ensures that attention is paid to every aspect of the venture (see Figure 5.1). The following key issues immediately become apparent.

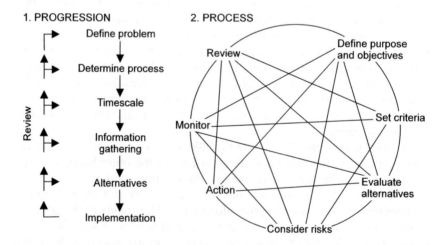

Purpose: to draw the distinction between the two elements of progress and process. The former is a schematic approach; the latter is that from which the former arises, and which refines it into its final format. Effective and successful decision-making requires the confidence that is generated by continued operation of the process.

Figure 5.1 *A decision-making model*

Time

This means addressing:

- Length of investment, whether short-, medium- or long-term; and above all, the actual lengths of time that are meant by each.
- Potential for time over-runs, and especially what this may imply for the ability to command finance, resources and technology; where this is a potential issue, arrangements for the financial and resource underwriting must be determined at the outset.
- Consequences for time under-runs: superficially, if something is completed early, it is extremely attractive all round. On the other hand, this may call into question the credibility of the planning and investment process. It may also cause some parties to investigate the quality of the finished work.
- Factors outside the venture's control: the potential for delays and time over-runs due to factors that cannot be precisely predicted or evaluated in advance of the venture must be addressed.
- knock-on effects: the knock-on effects on to other ventures, proposals and activities of time over-runs – for whatever reason, however good or bad – must be assessed in advance; in large and complex investments, this is certain to be a matter of concern to at least some of the parties (see box 5.1).

Box 5.1   *Timescales*

Football

At one end of the scale the football industry – especially at the upper end – is extremely short-term, driven by weekly results. Managers and coaches are given insufficient time to develop styles of play, players are transferred in and out, purely in the interests of short-term advantage. The industry is prepared to pay extremely heavily for this form of return in many instances. At the opposite end of the scale, the more forward-looking clubs have designed and implemented their own academies of excellence. This means that boys join what are effectively private schools from the age of eleven onwards. The purpose is twofold – to provide an excellent education; and to develop a football talent that has already been identified. Examples of clubs taking this approach include Manchester United (UK), Barcelona (Spain), Ajax and Feyenoord (Holland), AC Milan (Italy). These clubs also transfer players in and out.

This illustrates the complexity of investment in the particular industry; and also affords the clubs multiplicity of chances for success, although the actual basis on which the investment is made is of a very much greater order.

Post-It

The Post-It gummed paper pad was invented by a member of a church choir who wanted something that would mark the places in his hymn book for the duration of the church services in which he was singing and would not fall out when the book was first opened.

The matter became a personal obsession. It took twelve years to develop. However, once developed, it was commercialised by the 3M company. The company's investment was in the purchase of the prototype – the full development had been a matter for the individual. The company was able to put its full resources behind exploiting the product and used this to diversify into the office stationery supply sector.

Tarmac

In 1992 Tarmac plc, the UK construction and aggregates company, assessed its activity portfolio. Deciding that its main strength lay in its open-cast mining, quarrying and aggregates business, it sought ventures that would reinforce this and play to its perceived strengths elsewhere in the world. It acquired a controlling interest in a US open-cast coalmining company; and declared that this was a long-term venture, with the aim of securing a foothold in the open-cast mining and aggregates sector in North America.

During 1992 there were several changes in key personnel, and the direction was re-evaluated. The upshot was that the mining interest was sold on, barely 18 months after its acquisition, at a substantial loss.

These examples illustrate some of the complexities inherent in decision-making processes. It can also be inferred that:

- not all short-term investments are wrong (for example, many football clubs do buy instant success);
- not all long-term investment decisions are right (the Post-It would never have been developed if the interest of 3M or another company had not been engaged);
- these complexities reinforce the point made in the text above that this is a process and not a linear function.

Information

Except in the case of prescribed returns on deposits, it is not possible to have perfect information. The nearest thing is where a guaranteed minimum return is given at the outset of a venture, and even this can be lost if a particular party goes bankrupt, is taken over or changes overall direction. The problem is compounded by the propensity of those involved to fall back on, and to take as certain, financial projections and forecasts (see box 5.2).

Box 5.2   *The use and value of information*

In 1999, faced with falling sales and decline in reputation, the Co-operative Wholesale Society and the Cooperative Retail Society announced a partial merger. The result was to ensure that there was a concentration of resources on the part of the two organisations in the key areas of buying and distribution.

The two organisations emerged from the cooperative movement of the nineteenth century, which aimed to provide the basic commodities of life at affordable prices and to redistribute the trading surpluses in the form of 'dividends' – either paid in kind, in the form of free or cheap goods, or else cash vouchers which could be exchanged for goods.

In 1998 the Cooperative Retail Society acquired a new Chief Executive, Andrew Meehan, who declared his intention of reversing the declines in reputation and sales. He commissioned McKinsey, the management consultants, to come up with proposals for a shake-up. The result was to sell off the non-grocery parts of the business (46 department stores concerned with the sale of furniture and household goods) for £149 million. McKinsey also recommended that the Co-operative Retail Society and Cooperative Wholesale Society should merge in order to create a buying machine worth £4.5 billion per annum.

However, some issues remain unaddressed. If the venture is successful, the newly merged Cooperative Society is likely to attract takeover bids. The buying power of £4.5 million per annum looks an impressively large figure, but no set of criteria is published by the company as to whether it is good, mediocre, bad, effective or ineffective. Thirdly, Meehan himself is aware of the primary drives for the merger. Speaking in April 1999, he said 'The city machine – lawyers, advisers, bankers, the press – has a gargantuan appetite and it has to be fed'.

Nevertheless, the story was presented to both these parties, and the public at large as a venture from which both parties *would* gain, not one from which they *might* gain – or lose.

'Managements twist and turn as they search for a new story that will galvanise the analysts and elevate the price earnings ratio. One highly reliable ruse is to announce the sale of assets to concentrate on a new core. Divestment may well add one-off value simply by exploiting the markets and at low regard for the existing company and its management. Surgery is sometimes the only feasible remedy. Sell-off exercises often merely repair the devaluation wrought by past neglect of the real intrinsic worth of businesses however. Earnings are residuals, the result of effective or ineffective management, not only of costs and prices, but of every element in the whole business system'.

Source: The Times – 27 April 1999; Robert Heller, *Management Today*, December 1998.

Process

This means recognising the extent of influence, resources, drive and commitment on the part of all those involved, and gaining support for the venture in that context. It is quite usual for a powerful interest to override or carry along others who do not have the same clout; this nevertheless does not make it right (see box 5.3).

Alternatives

During the course of the decision-making process, alternatives become apparent to all those involved. The question then becomes whether the particular venture can continue to best satisfy the aims and objectives of those involved, or whether a new approach to the existing proposal is required, or whether it is best to search for fresh partners or other ventures. This is especially the case if it becomes apparent, in turn, that the matter in hand is no longer as attractive as once envisaged.

In decision-making, time, information, process and alternatives are interrelated. For example, there may not be enough time to gather adequate information before a decision is required; or it may be possible to gather better information later on. Alternatives may be acceptable to some of those involved but not to others, on the basis that they need more time to assess them. Information may be readily understood by some, but again may need more time for others. It can be extremely complex, yet needs to be worked through to the satisfaction of all concerned because the behavioural aspects have to be satisfied alongside the financial projections. However sound the proposal may be, if those involved are not personally and professionally convinced, they will not give their full support, and it will inevitably fall short of full success.

There are also other factors that have to be addressed.

Box 5.3 *Small investors and water privatisation*

The privatisation of the UK water industry in 1989 was wanted by no one except politicians and finance. At a time when the consumer drive was for a fully integrated national water grid distribution system, the industry was fragmented. However, the political expedient drive of raising substantial short-term funds, coupled with the medium-to-long-term prospects of extensive influence in the industry on the part of large corporations, overruled the operational priority.

Over the following five years, there were various occurrences. Attention was drawn to water quality, which was declining, and sewage management and dispersion, which was crude and basic. Eventually the water companies were given up to 15 years to remedy these matters. They were also allowed to charge customers and consumers additional premiums for future investment in quality and sewage dispersal.

The proposal was made superficially attractive by allowing a proportion of shares to be bought at discounted prices by individual consumers. At the end of the five-year period, however, these shares became available for compulsory purchase under the UK Companies Act 1988, which allowed anyone with more than a 90 per cent stakeholding in a company to acquire the remaining shares at the current market price. Small investors were therefore obliged to sell their shares on, under what was effectively a compulsory purchase order.

PROJECTIONS AND FORECASTS

The reason for engaging in projection and forecasting activities is so that the future can be faced with as much certainty as possible in the circumstances. Each depends upon the availability of high-quality and useable information for their accuracy and reliability.

Forecasting is a prediction of the future based on:

- knowledge and analysis of the present
- knowledge and analysis of the past

and relating the two to the set of circumstances immediately foreseen.

Forecasting further into the future is less certain. It requires acknowledgement that business and commercial circumstances change, and that operations and activities are affected by managers outside the venturer's control.

Projection is concerned with extrapolating the future based on current and historic statistics. Projections are produced by statisticians, economists and information scientists for use by managers in their decision-making processes. Projection is not a decision-making process in itself. These activities are then best supported through the use of the following modelling techniques.

Network Analysis

Network analysis is used to order and demonstrate the range of organisation scheduling, planning and control methods when devising the systems and processes necessary for the management of projects and ventures. The purpose is to identify in advance the shortest possible time in which these activities may be completed, and to identify those parts of the process that need to take place alongside the mainstream of activities (see Figure 5.2).

Blockage Analysis

Blockages occur because organisational systems operate at the speed of the slowest part. Once blockages are analysed they can then be plotted on the network diagram, as a precursor to assessing the best, medium and worst consequences of such blockages occurring.

This approach to projection and forecasting is used to evaluate likely, possible and potential outcomes of decisions (there are no certainties). This involves using the best information available and including all the behavioural, situational and environmental factors that may possibly have an effect (positive or negative) on the venture.

The great weaknesses of all forecasting activities are:

- The forecast becomes anticipated reality rather than informed, expert and, above all, *present* opinion of the outcome of something in the *future*.

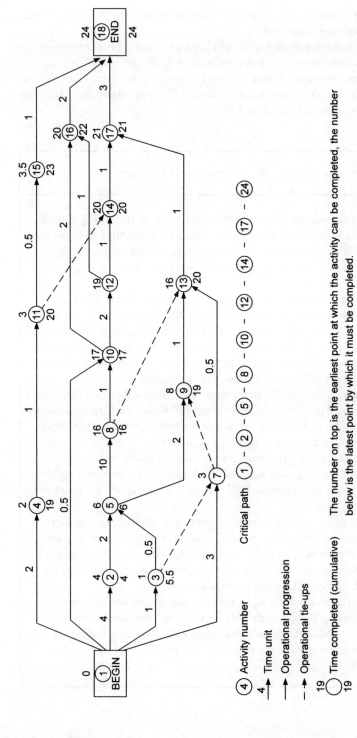

Activity number ④

Time unit ↑⁴

Operational progression →

Operational tie-ups ⤍

Time completed (cumulative) ⑲₁₉

Critical path ①–②–⑤–⑧–⑩–⑫–⑭–⑰–㉔

The number on top is the earliest point at which the activity can be completed, the number below is the latest point by which it must be completed.

Purpose: a project/operational schedule; a planning tool; a model against which to measure actual progress. Identification of critical incidents (those on the critical path). Identification of potential problems, blockages and hold-ups.

Figure 5.2 *A network diagram*

- The forecast gains a life of its own and becomes the basis on which everybody becomes involved.
- The forecast is used as a stick with which to beat those who implement the investment when returns do not measure up to projection.
- Any forecast, however good, is only remotely accurate so long as conditions in which it was made remain. If these change so does the validity of the forecast (see box 5.4).

Box 5.4   *The management of cash crises in universities*

In 1992 the government ordered UK universities to produce proposals for substantially increasing the numbers of students that they would admit. This put pressure on the existing resources of many British universities, and they were forced to seek alternative sources of funding.

Many universities sought fee-paying students from outside the European Union. In particular, full fee-paying students were attracted from the Far East. The economies of Japan, Singapore, Malaysia, Indonesia and the Philippines were booming. This had produced an extremely rich middle class in those countries, and its members now sought a Western education for the next generation.

Accordingly, many universities were able to attract students from these countries. They brought with them full fees, which ranged from £8,000 to £20,000 per student per undergraduate degree course. Many of the students were those whose parents were working in highly prestigious and highly successful and profitable industries.

Initially, the venture was successful all round. It came to a sudden and critical halt in October 1997 when the value of all of those currencies crashed.

The universities involved had thought that this ability to attract students from the Far East would guarantee their future for ever. Faced with the currency crash, some universities allowed undergraduates to remain for the duration of their courses and to pay what they could afford. Others cancelled the places.

This occurred overwhelmingly because the projection of a possible income-generating opportunity had been turned into eternal reality by the behaviour – not the financial management or investment appraisal – of those concerned with the ordering and direction of universities in Great Britain.

PRIORITIES

All parties bring their own priorities to a particular venture, as frequently stated. The venture has to be drawn up and modified if necessary so that these may be accommodated.

Two simple models of priorities can be used initially as follows:

(1) In which matters are prioritised; if circumstances change, those matters lower down the order of priority are cancelled;
(2) In which matters are prioritised; and if circumstances change, everything is attempted but nothing is satisfactory (see Figure 5.3).

It is therefore first necessary to know from which of these points of view those involved manage their priorities. Beyond that, it is essential to know what the individual priorities of those involved are (see box 5.5).

Complete openness is desirable. It nevertheless remains true that many priorities have to be inferred from the attitudes, behaviour and actions of those involved, because people are unwilling or unable to declare their true position. It is therefore necessary to be able to plan for changes in priorities; and the effects on the venture of such changes. This includes reference to effects of circumstances outside, as well as inside, the control of those involved (see box 5.6).

EXPERTS AND CONSULTANTS

Most practitioners in the financial services industry offer consultancy, advisory and executive services; and it is also true of merchant and clearing banks and finance houses. The following main issues need to be addressed.

- The reasons for hiring consultants and the results that they are required to produce.
- The purchase of expertise when required. Consultants do not increase overheads. They supply their expertise when required in return for fees. The hiring of consultants should be a short-term commitment designed to produce the desired results; and while this may, in the short term, appear an expensive approach, it becomes cost effective when:
  (a) the use of consultants is directly managed;
  (b) the commitment is indeed short-term (see box 5.7).

Box 5.5   *Illustration of priorities*

Even if understanding of, and commitment to, the particular venture is assumed, the following priorities have always to be understood and managed.

- *Politicians*: increased profile and prestige; career development and enhancement; representative interests; the priorities of their constituents; the party line.
- *Stockbrokers*: sale commissions; reputation; to increase the number of clients; to increase client returns.
- *Financiers*: to secure desired rates of return (whether or not these are achievable in the circumstances of a particular venture); to meet their internal objectives; to enhance reputation; to cover losses; to secure attractive investments and move funds on behalf of clients.
- *Pioneers and inventors*: to get their invention to market; to gain reputation; to increase profile; to secure funding for the next venture.
- *Technologists*: to enhance and improve reputation; to develop existing technology; to invent new technology; to commercialise technology; to be the best or the most highly regarded individual in the sector.
- *Growing companies*: to secure new ventures; to secure new markets; to maintain reputation; to address the consequences of slowdown in growth.
- *Shrinking companies*: to consolidate; to concentrate on the core; to maintain stock market confidence; to avoid loss of confidence.
- *Moribund companies*: when it becomes apparent that venturers are seeking or entering into arrangements with moribund companies, the first priority is to get those from that company to acknowledge that they are indeed suffering from inertia. The usual outputs of this are lengthy decision-making processes, and concentration on administration and procedure rather than results. When involved in ventures with such companies, a priority for the others involved is to break the inertia cycle.
- *Prestigious companies and brands*: maintenance and enhancement of brand strength and prestige; avoidance of ventures that may possibly damage brand strength and prestige.

Each of these points provides a useful focus for enquiry for those involved when seeking to assess the extent of priority to all concerned in the particular venture.

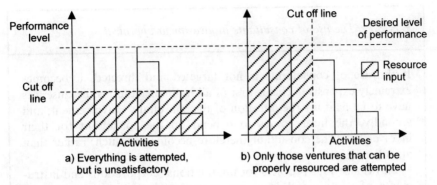

Figure 5.3 *Priorities*

Box 5.6 *Circumstances outside the control of venturers and priorities*

In summary, these are as follows.

- Changes in government economic policy, interest rates, currency values, rates of inflation.
- Changes in the political drive and nature of government; changes in the political constitution of government.
- Changes in taste and fashion.
- Changes in public perception and acceptability.
- Changes in technology and expertise.
- Changes in stock market and financial sector perception of good, bad, acceptable and unacceptable rates of return.
- Changes in personnel imposed on the venture by one or more of the parties causing the destruction of (or enhancement of) the existing relationship.

Notes

- Each of these may invalidate or destroy the value of an investment.
- Each of these may also enhance the value of an investment.
- Each of these may make it overvalued, causing some, but not all, parties to sell out and take profits while they can.
- Each of these may also create a set of circumstances that, in turn, creates demand for the outputs of the venture that cannot be satisfied. This causes initial high demand and overvalue of the product or service; and subsequently leads to sharp decline in value as those customers, clients and end-users who cannot avail themselves of the particular product or service seek their satisfaction elsewhere.

Box 5.7   *The use of consultants in investment appraisal*

If the use of consultants is not targeted and directed, it becomes extremely expensive. This is first of all in financial terms, because fees have to be paid for the duration of the consultant's involvement; and secondly, the hirer comes to depend on the consultant for their involvement. The consultant therefore becomes a crutch, rather than an enhancement.

This is a serious problem for multinational corporations and instruments of central and local government that engage in long-term expensive – and often unproductive – relationships with consultants. There is also a behavioural factor to be addressed, in that, because of the high fees charged (£2,500 per hour per consultant at Year 2000 prices is not uncommon) there is an overwhelming propensity to accept the consultant's recommendations, whether or not these are appropriate to the particular venture.

The problem is at its worst when, once the consultants are engaged, those concerned with the implementation of the venture are required to 'work with the consultants', or 'work according to the guidance of the consultants'. Specific aims and objectives require to be set if this is to be a productive relationship. Otherwise the result is as stated above – those directly involved come to depend on the consultants, rather than using them and their expertise to best advantage.

Investment appraisal and financial consultants are hired for any or all of the following reasons.

- To become more cost effective and efficient; to identify those areas in a venture where time or value may be lost; and time and value may be gained;
- To increase business volumes and output, again with reference to quantity, quality and time;
- To increase the efficiency and effectiveness of capital utilisation;
- To increase percentage rates of return, profit levels, turnover; to reduce costs, and charges;
- To improve image, reputation and confidence;
- To improve the use of technology and expertise;
- To attend to other organisational priorities – design, performance, regeneration, product and service management, marketing and sales.

It is unlikely that the effective use of consultants will fall outside these guidelines. Moreover, the precise way in which a particular problem is to be addressed needs definition, aims and objectives so that the particular situation is resolved according to the exact demands of the venture in question (see box 5.8).

Box 5.8 *Use of consultants in public services*

In 1988 a county council in southern England hired one of the top brand firms of financial and management consultants to 'redesign its organisation'. Working at the then agreed fee of £1,100 per hour, the consultants proposed a two-year investment programme. This would involve:

- the design, creation and implementation of a head office of 500 staff (previously this had 130 staff);
- redundancies, retraining and redeployment in frontline services; increase in workloads for teachers, librarians, social workers and highway maintenance staff;
- privatising and putting out to tender the management of basic amenities – especially security, cleaning and waste disposal;
- an aggressive stance to the trade union and other staff representatives involved.

In simple terms, the new corporate structure was to be paid for through cutting frontline services.

This was accepted by the particular county council. The venture was deemed to be 'highly successful' by all concerned. Accordingly, the consultancy firm was hired by another county council in the same area. The report produced for the second county council was identical in every aspect except that the names of places and key personnel had been changed.

While some financial and investment appraisal consultants are extremely good and willing to treat each venture on its own merits, it is important to be aware of the fact that others simply sell – often impose – only that with which they are familiar.

Investment appraisal consultants are used extensively to research the financial feasibility of proposals. They may do this for the whole proposal; or from the perspective of one or more, but not all, of those involved.

The latter needs caution. The consultants may have been hired for the best possible reasons. However, they may also have been hired to give a particular slant in the interests of the hiring party only. They may have been hired to give life to a bad proposal, or to kill off a good one, using their real or perceived expertise in the field to give a spurious rationale to the result required. Most insidiously of all, they may research the proposal on behalf of one client, and then offer their results to others who they know will pay more.

Investment appraisal consultants clearly have their place in arriving at investment decisions. Their own perspective on proposals, and the reasons and extent of their involvement, need to be understood in all cases.

OTHER INFLUENCES ON DECISION-MAKING

It is next necessary to consider the other influences that are brought to bear. These are always present to a greater or lesser extent, and the nature of their influence needs to be understood.

Key Players

These include the following.

- Key players – venture leaders including groups and committees
- Public interest, colloquy and acceptability
- Internal capability and acceptability
- Vested interests including trade unions, residents' associations, environmental, political and other pressure groups
- Influential players, individuals and groups
- Anyone who has a need for a quick result, triumph or prestige.

The position of these key players needs plotting on the knowledge–influence spectrum, and then managing accordingly. Otherwise the venture may become at risk, either from the force of their personality, or because of the dominant influence that they are able to exert in a particular situation.

Ethics

Ethics concerns the moral aspect of conduct and the rules and principles that govern it and that ought to govern it. Ethics in business is normally concerned with:

- maximising long-term owner and shareholder value. This, in turn, secures the optimum return on investment, and optimum value of the total venture. This is distinct from short-term gain and expediency which always dilutes ventures, and often leads to long-term institutional decline;
- ordinary common decency in dealings and treatment of all those involved.

Ethical dilemmas in investment appraisal normally concern:

- Reconciling advantages to one group of stakeholders at the expense of others.
- Reconciling the consumption of resources for packaging and presentation with the knowledge that these aspects make goods and services very much more marketable and therefore overtly profitable.
- Reconciling the wrong means to the right end. For example, it may be necessary to offer bribes to clients in order to secure work, and thereby ensure the future of those involved, and the jobs of those who have to carry out the work. This is an extensive dilemma in the oil, armaments, chemicals and waste management industries. There are many who also believe that vivisection in chemical and pharmaceutical research uses the wrong means to the right end.
- Reconciling the right means to the wrong end. This occurs for example, when investors make what is known to be a short-term investment in a company in order to make it immediately more attractive, and then sell it on for high levels of profit and advantage to shareholders.
- Reconciling the demand for products and services that generate waste and effluent that is damaging to the environment.
- Reconciling the production of morally unacceptable goods and services with the fact that they are in high demand and therefore make excellent financial investments. Armaments, defence equipment, pornography and tobacco products all fall into this category (see box 5.9).

Entry and Exit Barriers

Entry Barriers

Entry barriers are those hurdles that have to be jumped successfully when contemplating entering into new ventures. These are:

- *Technology*: concerned with the relative ease or difficulty of commanding, acquiring or purchasing technology and the expertise to use it.
- *Capital investment*: the total level of investment necessary to gain access to, and to sustain, profitable and effective activities. The extent of capital

required clearly varies between sectors. Account has also to be taken of required payback times, return on capital employed, opportunity costs and any alternatives.

- *Cost barriers*: including the level of cost to be incurred as a continuous long-term operator in the sector; and the consequent capacity of anyone involved in the venture to sustain this. It is necessary to recognise that cost premiums may be charged by those already operating in the sector to new players in order to cover their own uncertainties about them. This may be compounded if the new venture itself feels the need to bring their own cost and price advantages in order to be able to gain an initial foothold. It may therefore turn out that the new venture finds itself facing higher charges and reduced returns for the initial period of the operation; and these may have to be sustained into the medium- to long-term future.

- *Familiarity barriers*: venturers normally have to compete with the perceptions of permanent quality and reliability of established players in the field that they are seeking to enter. Other behavioural aspects are the more general norms and expectations of the sector and the ways in which business is conducted. Venturers have to be able to meet general standards of deadlines, delivery volumes, presentation and operations; or else they must be able to make their venture attractive in distinctive ways which transcend the existing approach.

- *Legal constraints*: all sectors have their own legal constraints as well as general duties (such as those concerned with employment practice, trading and financial standards). Some ventures require that specific partners are taken on as a condition of their going ahead; this is especially the case with cross-border ventures where the legislature of one country may insist on a local partner being involved.

- *Switching costs*: switching is the term given to the ability of venturers to move or switch from one sphere of activities to others. In general, switching costs are low when there is access to generic or multipurpose technology, and where no specialist attributes are required to make the proposed move. Switching costs are also low when there is a sufficient flexibility in the desired or required rates of return. Switching costs are high where there are political, economic, social and technological uncertainties; and where the costs of capital, currency exchange, interest and inflation rates are variable or uncertain.

- *The ability to differentiate*: in most cases, the outputs of ventures will not be unique; there is therefore the need to make these as attractive as possible to customers, clients and end-users in order to be able to set acceptable levels of charges to produce the desired rate of return.

- *Presentational factors*: as well as being acceptable, the proposal must be capable of being seen by all those involved as acceptable (see box 5.10).

Box 5.9 *Ethical investments*

Some financial services organisations offer 'ethical investment' to those who feel strongly that long-term, secure and profitable business can be conducted without compromising ethics. They undertake not to invest in anything that is deemed to be tainted by a lack of ordinary common decency in any aspect of the venture, or anything that is driven by expediency.

In practice, this is seldom possible. It is extremely hard to place funds in ventures or financial institutions that have no contact, support or investment themselves (direct or derived) in any areas that for whatever reason are deemed to be unwholesome.

It is also true that there exists still a strong belief and perception that striving for ethical purity is not possible; and there is certainly truth in this in those ventures that try everything in the pursuit of short-term gain.

Box 5.10 *The move of the Virgin company into airlines*

The Virgin Group of companies was founded on the success of ventures in the music production and retailing sectors. The move into airlines was first proposed by the company in 1982. In order for this to be achieved, entry barriers had to be addressed and cleared as follows.

- *Technology*: This consisted of the ability to purchase, maintain and service airliners, ticketing facilities, agency facilities, check-in and security aspects.
- *Cost barriers*: the ability to generate continuity of purchase of equipment, technology and facilities from suppliers already operating profitably and effectively with strong competitors, many of whom resented the entry of a high-quality, high-value niche operator into the sector.
- *Familiarity barriers*: The Virgin Group, and its founder and Chief Executive, Richard Branson, both enjoyed high-profile names and reputations. A key part of the investment process, however, had to be concerned with ensuring that the Virgin brand and reputation was enhanced by the airline venture rather than diminished; the latter would have led to questions of confidence in existing and familiar activities.

- *Behavioural aspects*: The approach taken by Virgin was to con-
sciously make the venture attractive in distinctive ways that trans-
cended the existing approach. This was mainly concerned with
attention to perceived added value in terms of the facilities on board
the airliners, and the extent of availability of airport services such as
pick-up and set-down facilities, exclusive lounges and waiting areas,
and ease of access to company representatives.
- *Switching costs*: In this venture, switching costs were relatively high.
While financial backing, and the ability to attract expertise were
available on the basis of confidence in the Virgin brand, suppliers of
technology especially, required to be convinced that the company
would indeed be able to pay for purchases made and to sustain these
payments.

A key part of the long-term and enduring success of the venture lies
in the fact that, prior to its proposed entry into the airline sector,
the company had neither experience nor expertise in the field. It
therefore set out to acquire this as a key part of the investment
process in order to ensure that the venture would be successful in the
long term.

Exit Barriers

The costs of withdrawing from a venture also have to be considered.

- *Costs*: Costs and charges are incurred as a result of ceasing operations and
activities. There are normally charges for withdrawing from ventures.
These may be as a result of penalty clauses; redundancy charges; sale of
assets at low prices; final payments; and any derived costs in terms of
losses and damages in other ventures and activities sustained as the result
of loss of confidence generated by withdrawal from the activity in
question.
- *Familiarity, confidence and reputation*: Where serious and general loss of
confidence would occur by withdrawal, this exit barrier is clearly very
high. Venturers therefore weigh up the effects of withdrawal from one
activity or range of activities in terms of the general effect on the rest of
their operations. Any organisation ceasing ventures in one sector needs to
do so without damage to its general reputation. Or withdrawal may take
place in such a way as to change wider perceptions of familiarity from
success to failure. Again, unless carefully managed, this may call into
question any confidence that exists in the total range of activities.

- *Destabilisation*: When withdrawing from a particular venture, those concerned need to assess the extent to which it may become destabilised. This may lead either to a total loss; or to merger or takeover activity in which the residual venture is normally bought up cheaply. Withdrawal of a key player may destabilise a whole sector, leaving a gap that becomes impossible to fill. The knock-on effects for others involved normally take the form of greatly reduced charges and greatly increased costs, again because of loss of faith that the sector is able to secure long-term viable returns.
- *Wastage and losses*: Most withdrawals are likely to lead to some wastage and loss. This becomes a problem if it creates difficulties related to disposal; assets may lose value to such a point that they have to be written off altogether.

The assessment of entry and exit barriers is therefore a key part of the information-gathering process. It gives a fresh outlook on the potential for success or failure of particular ventures. When deciding to go ahead with a particular venture, it is essential to recognise that the decision to proceed brings with it additional costs and charges (see box 5.11).

Box 5.11   *Other aspects of entry and exit*

Depending on the particular venture in question, the following may be seen either as entry or exit barriers.

- *Teething troubles*: Teething troubles are a barrier to entry, or at least to further progress, when, for whatever reason, their full extent has not been understood or costed. In practice, very few ventures do not have teething troubles that have to be underwritten after the point of decision to proceed. However, if these are either expensive or critical, some venturers may seek to withdraw. This also applies to production of prototypes, models and pilot ventures, which again throw up unforeseen problems or charges.
- *Markets*: Changes in nature, levels and volumes of market activities may either enhance or diminish the attractiveness of ventures. For example, a venture that had the original aim of creating its own market or niche may find itself having to draw customers and end-users away from existing products and services. Or ventures that were designed for capturing markets from existing players may generate levels of interest independent of the existing players. Each of these has consequences for the pressures inherent in the venture,

and the demands placed on it, both by financiers and backers, and also customers, clients and end-users.

- *Opportunity costs*: There is always the danger that those with limited resources will be asked to become involved in ventures that appear – or are – more attractive than those currently in hand, a short way after the decision has been taken to go ahead. The problem of switching costs, withdrawal costs, and any loss or damage to reputation and confidence, has always to be addressed when this occurs.

- *Asset values*: The value placed on assets is often subjective, and this always needs to be understood when calculating returns on investment or returns on capital employed as a consequence of becoming involved in a venture. Organisations re-value and devalue their assets in order to present them to best advantage on balance sheets; when appraising investment proposals, this is the context in which real asset values need to be seen.

CONCLUSIONS

At first sight, much of this looks either obvious or else a very heavy-handed way of arriving at a point at which all those involved can agree the best way to proceed. It is quite true that the process should be conducted as quickly and as effectively as possible. It does however need to be thorough.

As long as everyone involved is coming into the venture with sufficient knowledge, understanding, expertise and confidence, the process need not take long. Most of it in fact will have been carried out in the past while gaining the required expertise, and as a result of experience in previous ventures.

It all needs to be covered in some way however, if effective investment decisions are to be taken. Those going into the venture can then do so with full confidence that what has been decided has the unqualified support of everyone involved. If there are any waiverers, the different parts of the process are designed to ensure that sufficient clarity of direction, information and purpose is gained. This either means that the doubters have their reservations removed; or else it means that their doubts are clarified to such an extent that they withdraw from the venture (see box 5.12).

Going through such a process also enables a line of reasoning to be established so that everyone is clear how and why the decision was arrived at as well as what was agreed. It also serves as a major means of checking the quality and effectiveness of the decision-making process when it becomes necessary to measure progress.

Box 5.12 *Doubters*

Dealing with doubters can be very frustrating, especially when the benefits of a particular venture are apparent to everybody else!! It is therefore very easy for those who have no doubts to begin to tell the doubters what they want to hear (rather than what they need to hear) in order to speed up the decision-making process and gain commitment to purpose.

This rarely works. It is better to recognise at the outset that there are likely to be such problems to be faced. Time can then be built into the process to tackle them. This should include 'emergency time', enabling other backers or venturers to be sought if someone hitherto involved drops out.

There are also legal constraints. In the personal financial services industry, all sales and ventures have to have a 14-day cooling-off period written in to them; and at any point during this period the potential investor may withdraw without penalty or loss of reputation.

The same applies to commercial ventures. Corporate backers may not be drawn into ventures, nor may they manipulate them for their own purposes. Venturers are not allowed to buy or sell shares in such a way as to enhance or diminish their value, and therefore to make an investment more or less attractive. In 1986 four of the members of the Board of Directors of Guinness plc were convicted of manipulating the share price of the company in order to enhance its value during a proposed takeover bid. This was in response to the fact that, while the company was seen to be an attractive target for takeover investment, it had been too highly valued. The directors therefore sought to drive up the price of the shares in order to make it seem more attractive, and therefore to allay the doubts of those who were still not sure.

6   Investment Measurement

INTRODUCTION

This part of the investment process is rarely carried out adequately. In particular, corporate investments that go wrong are not reviewed or evaluated. Those involved prefer to rely on bland and meaningless phrases such as 'adverse market conditions', 'difficult trading circumstances' or 'political instability', rather than conducting thorough analysis. This point is of particular concern because any real nod in the direction of adequate pre-investment appraisal would have identified these factors in these terms, and should therefore have become key points of enquiry.

Investments that succeed also need the same thoroughness to be applied. This is so that lessons can be learned in order to inform future investment decisions. Measurement, review and evaluation all start from a simple set of premises, as follows.

- *Purpose*: What did we set out to achieve? Did we achieve it? If so, why? If not, why not? Were there other sub-purposes, aims and objectives, and if so, were these achieved; and if so, why; and if not, why not?
- *Success*: In whose terms and why? Who says so and why? On what grounds and by whom is success being claimed?
- *Failure*: Again, in whose terms and why? On what grounds and why?
- *Opportunities*: What other opportunities became apparent along the way? Were these taken up? If so, why, and what happened? If not, why not?
- *Consequences*: What were, are and will be the consequences of undertaking the particular venture? Were there opportunity costs and opportunities forgone as a result? What other areas of activity have been opened up?
- *Keys*: Were there any single events, attributes or personalities on which the success or failure of the venture hinged? If so, what were these? What are the implications for future ventures?

Nevertheless, it remains very quick and easy to give partial and superficial answers to all these points and then move on to the next venture without having learned anything (see box 6.1).

Box 6.1 *WalMart takeover of Asda, 1999*

This is clearly and obviously a fantastic success! The initiative was announced in July 1999. This followed extensive adverse publicity alleging high prices in British supermarkets that compared unfavourably with both mainland Europe and North America. This venture, so it was widely agreed, will therefore bring prices down at Asda; and therefore force the other big supermarket retailers to cut their prices too.

Asda directors and shareholders' representatives agreed to the takeover and it went through. Customers are looking forward to spending less. Media, financial and retail analysts have all given their seal of approval. What can possibly go wrong?

This is the normal depth of investment analysis and measurement that is conducted. Superficially extremely attractive, it nevertheless entirely fails to address the following key questions, each of which needs to be satisfied if the investment is to succeed, and to be seen to succeed, from the point of view of everyone involved.

Initially, it was taken on trust that WalMart would indeed use the venture to drive down prices in the UK groceries market. The other possible alternatives were simply not considered. In particular, nobody considered the case that the venture might be primarily a property investment. Neither did anyone give consideration to the fact that WalMart might be seeking to enter what for them would be a high-price, high-margin niche.

In the United States, WalMart has always based its commercial successes on high-volume, low-margin sales. Equivalent ventures in the UK (e.g. Netto, Aldi) have so far gained a small foothold only, and have not taken market share away from the big supermarkets. Sainsbury's, the biggest loser of customers over the period 1995–2000, have largely lost these to Tesco and Asda, and not to low-price alternatives.

The costs and charges incurred, both initially and continuing, in the UK are different from those in the USA. The cost base is structured differently. Distribution methods are different. No in-depth assessment had been carried out by analysts to try and establish what would happen if the company found itself unwilling or unable to sustain these costs.

No analysis was carried out with a view to establishing the effect on premium and high-demand products and brands in the UK (e.g. Coca-Cola, Heinz). The company has no history in managing and distributing UK domestic brands (e.g. HP, Tetley), nor does it have an established commercial relationship with them.

The company has not declared its own specific objectives in moving into the UK supermarket sector. Discussion of the venture has been limited solely to the points made in the first paragraph.

Source: University College London, 1999; Retail Industries
　　　　 Consortium, 1999.

MEASUREMENT VERSES FORECASTS

Clearly, therefore, something better is required. The first step is to establish the means by which real progress can be measured against forecasts and projections. This, in turn, means that forecasting has to be conducted in ways that enable measurement to be made, as shown in Figure 6.1.

This can then be given a broader context by using a 'what if?' approach as in Figure 6.2.

The information thus presented can then be assessed against the precise demands and expectations of shareholders, backers, venturers and other stakeholders. So the whole process looks as shown in Figure 6.3.

This approach at least requires those concerned with designing, managing and maintaining investment ventures through to completion, to consider the full context; and that they understand that there is a full context to consider rather than merely a narrow dominant interest. It also requires a considered approach to forecasting rather than accepting with enthusiasm projections of success as absolute fact (see box 6.2).

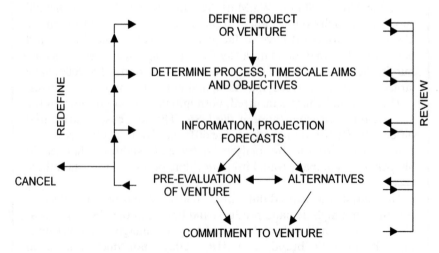

Figure 6.1   A simple measurement and forecasting model

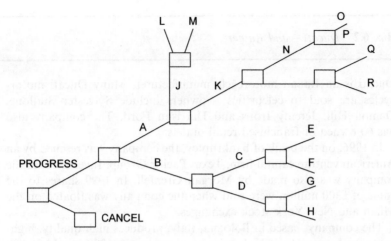

Purpose: To illustrate proposed courses of action, and likely and possible outcomes of them, from a given starting point. In this particular example, option X – CANCEL – is evidently not on the agenda, as the consequences of this are not extrapolated. What is illustrated are the ramifications that accrue once the decision is taken to progress; and assuming two positive choices (i.e. other than cancellation) at each stage. The tree is a useful illumination of the complexity and implications of the process, and of the reality of taking one decision.

Figure 6.2 '*What if?' approach: the decision tree*

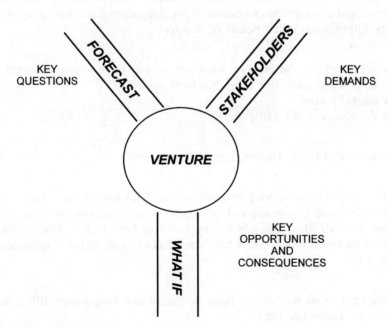

Figure 6.3 *The complexity of measurement*

Box 6.2   *Ducati – and Ratner*

Ducati is an Italian motorcycle manufacturer. Many Ducati motorcycles are sold to celebrities – owners include Sylvester Stallone,
Damon Hill, Jeremy Irons and Harrison Ford. The company also
has 60 owned or franchised retail outlets.

In 1996, on the brink of bankruptcy, the company was rescued by an
American venture capital firm, Texas Pacific Group. Investment in the
company was also made by Morgan Grenfell. In 1999 shares to the
value of £300 million were sold when the company was floated on the
Milan and New York stock exchanges.

The company, based in Bologna, Italy, produces high-quality, high-
value, high-reputation, high-price motorcycles. In 1998 it sold 30,000
motorcycles. This represented sales of £162 million, compared with
£130 million in 1996; and this caused the company's Chief Executive,
Frederick Minoli, to claim that the company was now 'the most
profitable motorcycle company in the world'.

Financial journalists and media analysts hailed the rejuvenation of
the company to be a great success. However, other than a nod in the
direction of the fact that the company has been rescued from bankruptcy, no basis for this success or failure is established. So anyone
interested in establishing a rationale for this judgement is left only with
the following as initial points of enquiry:

- sales volume and income; the basis on which 'the most profitable
  motorcycle company' claim has been made;
- celebrity sales;
- the numbers of retail outlets.

Source: F. Minoli, Ducati Annual Report 1999.

'If you don't over extend yourself, if you don't overpay for staff and
facilities, and if you are not willing to borrow heavily to make up
the shortfall, then you are not regarded as hip or chic. That is the
basis on which people either have confidence in you, or lose confidence
in you'.

Source: Gerald Ratner, speaking on the *Money Programme*, BBC, 30
         December 1989.

SUCCESS AND FAILURE

Success and failure are subjective value judgements placed by people on all activities including investment (see box 6.3).

It is essential to understand at the outset how each of the participants is going to judge the venture for success or failure. This is especially important where there is a dominant interest because the other players may be forced to modify their own expectations.

The consequences of failure also need to be addressed. If a key or dominant venturer feels that, as the initiative has progressed, they have little or no chance of success, they may pull out. This has serious, often fatal, consequences for the future of the venture. The issue therefore needs defining precisely, together with the full consequences of failure for everyone involved. These need to be clearly understood and accepted by all concerned before a venture is undertaken.

KNOWLEDGE AND UNDERSTANDING

When a venture is being put together, approach is initially made to those with knowledge and understanding in the proposed field of activity. Clearly, however, it is not always possible to use those experienced and expert in the field, and so others have to be persuaded to translate either their expertise or their finance into new areas.

This is often accelerated by regional development initiatives, or other grants and enhancements from such bodies as national governments, the UN, EU, NATO and World Bank. Superficially, it can be very attractive to become involved, knowing that the costs of the venture are being wholly or largely underwritten; and this is compounded if minimum profit margins are also guaranteed.

Complete knowledge and understanding does however require a broader assessment. Other costs that have to be considered include:

- Human costs concerning the consequences of relocating staff from their familiar environment elsewhere, especially for long periods of time, or else in areas of political turmoil (see box 6.4).
- Hidden costs, especially the real operational costs in other areas of the world where, for example, it may be necessary to use bribes and inducements; or the costs of time delays caused by logistical problems. In unfamiliar sectors in a familiar location, new players may find themselves at the mercy of pressures from the existing dominant players. This happened to Virgin Atlantic, for example, when it was trying to negotiate routes and airport landing slots and rights for itself in the face of intense pressure from British Airways, American Airlines and other major established international players.

- Maintenance, replacement and improvement costs which may not be fully clear at the outset;
- Costs brought about by delays, time lags and other aspects of 'venture drift'.
- Competitor costs, especially when these are reduced. This applies especially to information and technology projects and research where venturers can be threatened by the activities of a dominant player (e.g. Microsoft in the computer software industry). Threats also come from fresh inventions by competitors that enable the required job to be carried out more cheaply and/or to a better quality or shorter timescale.

This indicates the context in which investment performance is measured effectively. Specific measures then need to be drawn up so that precise evaluation can take place. Quantitative and qualitative measures are used.

Quantitative Measures of Performance

These are used against projections and forecasts; and against expectations; and in the context indicated above, as follows.

- *Return on investment*: in whatever precise terms that was stated; in terms acceptable to the parties to the venture; and in terms acceptable to the venture itself.
- *Cash flow*: including inflow and outflow balances; and with especial reference to hidden costs (e.g. overdraft and contingency fund provisions) that subsequently become necessary.
- *Income, expenditure, profit and loss*: each of these can be calculated in simple format as follows:
  - per employee – this should include all the employees involved in the particular venture; and not just those at the sharp end or frontline;
  - per customer, client or end-user – by which the totals over the period of the venture are measured against the numbers of customers and clients;
  - per product or service – either on an individual, product mix or product range basis;
  - per outlet – in whatever terms the outlet is defined by those involved (e.g. offices; sales people; department stores; airliners; ships; restaurants);
  - per square foot, per square metre – of especial value when capital is tied up in the acquisition and maintenance of property and facilities;
  - per location – having regard to the relative levels of prosperity, disposable income and propensity to spend of local client bases served.
- *Derived income, cost, profit and loss*: each of these elements as being derived or consequential; this is especially important when resources are drawn into one venture at the expense or to the detriment of others.

Box 6.3 *Different perceptions of success and failure*

Simple

- Success: I was only 20 minutes late
- Failure: I was 20 minutes late and I'm sorry
- Justified: I was 20 minutes late because the train broke down

Complex (translated into investment measurement)

- Success: I got 20 per cent return on my investment in six months
- Failure: I only got 20 per cent return on my investment in six months
- Justified: I got 20 per cent return on my investment in six months because this was a good/bad venture.

Stakeholder view of success and failure (simplified)

Example: depleted uranium artillery

- Politicians: it is cheap and affordable.
- Military: it is very effective and destructive.
- World governments: we want it also; we need it also.
- Defence contractors: if we can make this equipment, our future is assured.
- Defence sales people: if we can sell this equipment, our future is assured.
- Inventors and technologists: the opportunity to work at the leading edge of military research; the potential for developing the technology into other areas.
- Environmental: the toxic residue lasts for millions of years
- Public colloquy and acceptance: we beat the enemy because of our superior firepower (reinforced by media coverage).
- Public revulsion: we're suffering radiation sickness for an unknown length of time, and for an unknown number of generations.
- Justified: we started the war; we defeated the dictator; if we didn't use it then it would be sold elsewhere and used against us.

At best, this is a self-justification approach to success and failure, and therefore remains almost entirely subjective and partial.

Source: *Tonight*, produced by Michael Nicholson, ITV Carlton, 25 August 1999.

Box 6.4   *Water contracting in Chechnya*

In 1997, following the end of one round of the enduring civil war in Chechnya between those who wished to form an independent state and the Russian authorities then responsible for governing the region, a water engineering project was commissioned. The contract was awarded to Southern Water plc, and a part of the work was awarded to Technics Ltd., a specialist water consultancy operating out of Guildford, Surrey.

The project was underwritten by both the EU, and the World Bank – both of whom wished to see the conflict in Chechnya ended, and saw, as one way forward in achieving this, the commissioning of work that would improve the all-round quality of life.

Technics' involvement in the project was destroyed when three members of its staff working in Chechnya were first taken hostage and then murdered by a group of people fighting for independence for the region.

The company was paid off in full by the EU and World Bank. Other subcontractors were subsequently appointed. The fee levels commanded were very much higher and the work proceeded on the basis of complete anonymity.

Financial measures may also be expressed in terms of the following.

- *Volume sales*: per product, per product cluster, per product range; volume sales per square foot, per square metre, per outlet; volume sales per member of staff may also be calculated and again, this should include everyone directly employed. In many cases, this will also include those in derived employment – having been drawn into the particular venture and away from other duties.
- *Density/frequency of usage*: this especially applies to sports, health care, hotel facilities, public transport, bank cash points, commercial durables such as photocopiers and faxes, as well as to supermarkets and retail outlets.
- *Longevity of usage*: this can usefully be applied to private transport, public transport, consumer durables, clothing, furniture and white goods.
- *Speed of turnover*: the frequency with which the outputs of the venture are turned over, and it indicates the level of finance necessary to support the requirements to keep everything fully stocked.

- *Percentage calculations*: it is useful to note different percentage calculations, especially costs as a percentage of total income; percentage levels of profit; percentage returns on investment and capital employed. Their best use is to indicate levels of business necessary to sustain effective, successful and profitable ventures. Their worst use is when they become driving forces for performance targets without being set in their full context.

A model for the measurement of investment performance may now begin to be drawn up (see Figure 6.4).

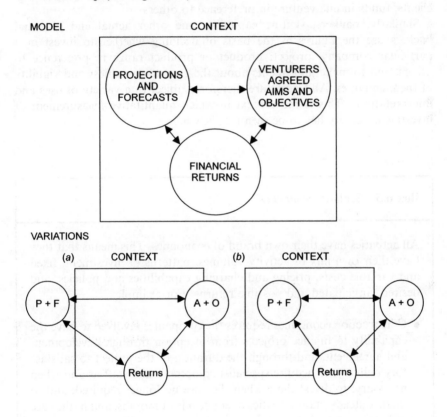

Notes
(a) *Likely to fail*: projections and forecasts are taken outside the context of the venture itself; venturers' aims and objectives are only partly sustainable in context; the financial returns also are only partly achievable in the context.
(b) *Likely to fall short of full success*: venturers' aims and objectives not fully placed in context; forecasting and projection has taken place in context; financial returns are heavily dependent upon the accuracy of forecasts and projections because no reference has been made to the broader context by the venturers.

Figure 6.4   *A model for the measurement of investment performance*

All venturers should – and do – produce mathematical, statistical and financial information in support of their ventures. It should be apparent, however, that this is not an end in itself. How this information is used, who uses it and for what reasons are of equal importance. The need to understand what the figures and numbers indicate is therefore vital, and this varies between the different interested parties.

In particular, stock market analysts use these measures of performance to predict the future performance of their interests in public companies. They also use this information to decide whether or not to invest their own, and clients, funds in one venture in preference to others.

Similarly, bankers, venture capitalists and other actual and potential backers use the figures as the basis of deciding whether to invest in a particular company, project, product or product range in preference to others, and to make judgements about the general soundness and viability of these activities. All figures are therefore subject to a variety of uses and interpretations. This is the context in which quantitative measurement of investment activity has to be seen (see box 6.5).

Box 6.5   *Sectoral economics*

All activities have their own brand of economics. This means that they have their own mix of activity volumes, patterns of investment, fixed and variable costs, pricing and charging capabilities and policies, and desired, anticipated and possible returns. For example:

- Construction economics requires the companies involved to have the capability to finance projects from inception through development and agreement, and through the duration of the project to satisfactory delivery; to acquire specialist equipment and staff as and when necessary; to divest these when they are no longer required; and to finance steady-state activities over periods of months, and in the case of large or complex projects, many years.
- Health economics requires organisations to have the capability to fund health care and development over indeterminate periods of time; to acquire specialist equipment; to acquire the products and outputs of medical research – drugs, treatments, technology – as and when necessary or desired; to contribute to health research and advancement.
- Corner shop economics requires the ability to satisfy large volumes of small purchase customers; to acquire and present a range of

products to sustain this; to generate sufficient cash flow in the short term to enable stocks to be replenished.

- Brand economics requires the ability to command flexible, financial and resource bases, often at very short notice. This is so that competitive responses can be made, as well as the undertaking of competitive initiatives; and it may be essential that short-term, high-quality competitive responses are made if a sudden and effective move by a competitor causes a quick downturn in demand and income.

Financial strength is therefore further assessed by relating the features of the particular backgrounds and sectors of those organisations that wish to operate in them, and by recognising the opportunities and constraints present.

All financial and statistical information must be capable of being used by those responsible for the conception, commitment and delivery of particular ventures. This means that:

- Historic and current information has to be complete and accurate, and both the information itself, and also the methods used to collect, store, retrieve and present it, must be suitable for the purposes of those who are to use it.
- All quantitative data is only of value if it is available in ways in which those responsible for the direction and measurement of investment ventures can understand and use it.
- Everyone concerned in the particular venture must have faith and confidence in the quality of information received, the systems used, and its presentation.

Qualitative Measures of Investment Performance

Effective attention to the qualitative aspects of the measurement of investment performance is essential if the matters relating to subjectivity indicated above are to be fully addressed. This means ensuring effective qualitative attention to all aspects of the performance of the venture; and providing distinctive measures of success and failure by which it will be judged.

Levels of Performance

Two main levels of investment performance may be distinguished.

- *Steady-state*: conducting and organising ventures in regularised ways.
- *Crisis*: anticipating and handling problems and unexpected incidents and occurrences.

Other levels may also be identified.

- *Pioneering*: innovation, creativity, invention and development.
- *Policy*: setting standards of behaviour and performance.
- *Maintenance and improvement*: seeking opportunities that become apparent throughout the venture; with particular reference to expertise and technology usage; improving the quality of communications, administration and management systems; improving the quality and performance of products and services; improving the marketing, sales and presentational factors.

At the outset of ventures, the proposed activities should be assessed under each of the above headings. Progress and effectiveness can then be measured during the period of the particular venture, and the differences and similarities between projections and reality noted.

Traditionally three levels of investment performance are distinguished.

- *Unsatisfactory*: remedied as and when it occurs.
- *Excellent*: high levels of return on investment and on capital employed; high levels of output, quality and satisfaction.
- *Satisfactory*: achieved (or assumed to be achieved) by some ventures over long periods; reflected in 'adequate' levels of profit, return on investment, success and effectiveness (and often not measured any more deeply).

This gives a slightly different approach to providing a basis on which subjective judgements may be deepened and made more substantial. If the unsatisfactory/excellent/satisfactory approach is used, then each requires precise definition at the outset of the particular venture.

Either of these approaches then sets a basis on which the qualitative aspects of investment performance can be measured. It needs to consist of a series of regularised formal reviews at which targets and objectives are discussed and assessed for success and failure. This also helps to form a continuous relationship between all those involved that both builds confidence and understanding, and enables particular issues and problems to be identified early. The process must be flexible and dynamic, and participative.

The qualitative aspects of performance measurement may fall into disrepute for the following reasons.

- If they are neither believed in nor valued; if they do not contribute to the wider success of the venture.
- If they are bureaucratic or mechanistic, rather than targeted and progressive.
- If the reviews are too infrequent or missed altogether; or they become a procedural meeting attended by junior functionaries only.
- They also suffer if measurement and performance criteria are identified in general terms only. This leads to misconceptions, inconsistencies, unevenness, and a lack of understanding of what the outputs are supposed to be; and this leads on again to cultures of blame, and disproportionate influence being accorded to dominant players.

In order for effective investment measurement to take place, the following components also need to be present.

- Disclosure of information in terms of volume, quality and honesty;
- The nature of involvement of all the parties concerned;
- The nature of any political involvement and also that of vested interests and pressure groups;
- Attention to the moral components of investment policy and purposes;
- The range of concerns that ought to be considered by those involved;
- Attention to the public interest, public lobbies and pressure groups; and where necessary, steps taken to manage these;
- The maximisation of long-term venturer interest.
- Ordinary common decency.

This is a highly qualitative and subjective checklist. However, all those concerned should be aware that these matters must be addressed if successful ventures are to be contemplated. Those ventures that do lead to long-term and enduring success do so because the broadest possible perspective on the measurement of performance has been considered.

The Measurement of Performance in Public Services

The main problem to be addressed lies in the establishment of a valid standpoint from which to measure the performance of these ventures. This has to be reconciled with the immediate short-term needs, drives and directions of politicians and service managers. There are also often historical bases, resource constraints and social pressures which all have to be accommodated.

The knowledge, expertise, judgement, attributes and qualities of those involved in the venture become critical. These form the context in which the broad and narrow perspectives can be taken as follows.

- *Broad*: state of the finished venture – whether school, classroom, library, hospital ward, laboratory or prison; the availability used to value quality and appropriateness of equipment to service users and consumers. Cleanliness, warmth and comfort; general ambience; professionalism of staff; currency of professional expertise; interaction of staff with client bases; prioritisation of activities; resource effectiveness, efficiency, adequacy and usage; quality, durability and strength of finished facility.
- *Narrow*: the ability to apply absolute standards of service delivery; speed of response to clients; nature and content of response to clients; nature and volume of complaints, failures and shortcomings; attitudes of service users to providers and vice versa; acceptance of professional responsibility for standards; acceptance of professional development; professional and personal commitment; attention to quality, maintenance and improvement of service.

This provides the context for setting specific aims, objectives and targets in public service investments. It requires concentration on the output of specific services, rather than reference to inter-functional comparisons or league tables. Those that are forced to attend to inter-functional comparisons and league tables at least know the fundamental weakness from which they are being asked to invest. It is therefore essential that the effective delivery of public service ventures depends on the availability of public sector professional expertise, and the ability to reconcile their expert judgement with the demands of the venture.

INVALID AND INAPPROPRIATE MEASUREMENTS

Invalid and inappropriate measurements are used to measure the success or failure of ventures from the point of view of partiality, expediency or ignorance.

The most commonly used are:

- *Retail price indices and inflation rates*: As a measure of performance, this takes no account of whether this is a good or bad return in sectoral or venture terms; nor does it indicate whether or not better or worse returns could have been gained from investing elsewhere.
- *Interest rates*: especially those relating to returns on deposit accounts and overdrafts. Again, in isolation, this takes no account of whether or not this is an adequate return; or, in the case of overdraft rates, whether this is an effective use of funds.
- *Use of accounting conventions*: to determine product costs, on-costs, overheads as an investment factor rather than operational baseline. This

becomes a serious problem when the demands of accounting functions are allowed to sway the overall appraisal of a particular investment.

- *Demands of the annual report*: especially to determine annual cost and profit percentages. While the production and delivery of the annual report in accordance with accounting conventions is a legal requirement, this requires total separation from the costing and measurement of the operation of the ventures.

Demands of Internal Markets

Internal markets are present in complex ventures and holding company structures, multinational organisations, as well as health and other public services. They are a combination of the following elements.

- The distinction between purchasers and providers for the purposes of establishing a contracted internal arrangement.
- The establishment of a contracted agreement between purchasers and providers as the basis on which the relationship between the two is to be carried out in the future.
- The establishment of a price–service return, and the ways in which the services are to be paid for.
- The establishment of a system of transfer pricing which enables the most advantageous currency or pricing formula to be used; and in public service organisations, requires a system of internal invoicing to be devised. This becomes a serious problem when notional asset and liability values used in accounting conventions become the basis for deciding whether or not investment can be avoided in a particular venture.

Public Services

It is especially important to be aware of the following when investing in public service ventures. These demands are usually placed by politicians and public service governors for their own, often self-serving, purposes.

- *Health*: In health care ventures, a means of calculating returns on investment have been neither devised nor agreed. The most insidious methods used are: cost per patient; cost per bed (hospitals); cost per activity (health checks, scans, eye checks); frequency and density of usage of equipment charges. Those involved in investing in health care ventures for the public service and National Health Service are at especial risk of having their costings, charges and returns varied according to political whim and expediency, and the peculiar approach is taken by public service budget setters (see box 6.6).

- *Education*: The most insidious measures of performance that are used are: lifetime costs of facilities; cost per pupil/student; usage charges for facilities (see box 6.7).
- *Defence contracting*: The most insidious measures of investment in this field stem from the fact that the approach that is taken is 'distributive' or based on a 'collective bargain'. There is a history and tradition in the defence, contracting and procurement industries that requires the contractor to go in with far too high a bid for work; and conversely, the government to deliberately under-price what is required. From this, an agreement is reached somewhere between the two extreme points. This is endemic throughout the whole sector and includes defence research projects, as well as the design and building of hardware (see box 6.8).
- *Infrastructure*: The measurement of performance of infrastructure projects is most vulnerable to such subject approaches as bonuses for early completion, and quality assurance concerns. In particular, bonuses for early completion of these facilities led to corners in projects deliberately being cut, either through the use of substandard materials, or else carrying out work in conditions that are known to have an adverse effect on the future performance of the facility (see box 6.9).
- *Other political aspects*: Privatisation and private finance initiative activities, especially, leave investors vulnerable to ultimate reception by end-users. While some ventures may have seemed overwhelmingly attractive at the outset, the results can be very different (see box 6.10).

Box 6.6 *Health care investment*

The British Union of Patients' Associations (BUPA) is a leading provider of private medical care in the UK. In October 1999 it announced a series of fixed-cost medical services and operation provisions that were open to all members of the public provided they could pay the charges. BUPA was able to do this because it had resources, equipment and expertise that were not being fully utilised; the venture therefore carried both commercial advantage and also enhancement and broadening of the service.

In the same month, in south-eastern England, four Health Care Trusts announced that they were closing wards and hospital beds because they could no longer afford to keep them open. At the same time, specialist equipment was to be rationed in its usage; and one brain scanner was to be closed from October 1999 to April 2000, despite the fact that this would lead to a worse quality of treatment, longer waiting lists and, inevitably, to more serious operations being required in the future.

The basis on which the latter case was arrived at was that it was cheaper to close wards than to keep them open; and cheaper to have expensive equipment lying idle than being used.

Box 6.7 *Education charges*

The Education Service Accounting Convention requires that, whenever a classroom, library or computer facility is not in use, no charge is made against it. However, the moment that it comes into use, it is charged to the service as if it is a brand new facility and has to be fully written down. Rather than looking at the marginal revenue that could be accrued by making reasonable charges to those wishing to use the facilities at times when the schools are not operational, these institutions have priced themselves out of the market by charging:

- £63.00 per usage for a school football pitch for a Sunday morning football club;
- £70.00 per usage for classroom facilities for post-school activities;
- £120.00 per usage for adult evening classes;
- £44.00 per usage for a cub-scout group.

All of these prices were quoted by a college in the Canterbury area of south-eastern England when it was asked to provide these facilities. None of these ventures came to pass.

Box 6.8 *Advanced Warning Aerial Command System (AWACS)*

The Advanced Warning Aerial Command System was commissioned in order to upgrade the effectiveness of the capability to detect hostile aircraft and submarines during the Cold War. First commissioned in 1975, it came partially into service in 1992, and by 1997 it was recognised and agreed that it would never be fully operational in the ways intended.

Part of the reason for this was that global circumstances had changed. The Cold War effectively ended in 1988. However, the equipment also proved ineffective in dealing with non-military issues such as sea rescues, the location of oil slicks, and bad weather. It also proved difficult to apply to the military circumstances in which it was required to operate once it did become at least partially operational. In particular, it made a negligible contribution to the conflict in Kosovo in 1999, when an accurate military detection plane would have been invaluable in targeting precisely military facilities (admittedly land-based) that needed to be attacked as part of the process of resolving the political situation in southern Yugoslavia.

The project was a joint venture between the governments of the UK and USA. The main contract was awarded to Boeing and Lockheed Martin; technology contracts were awarded to GEC, Plessey, and Racal. In 1975 the venture had a capital worth of £63 million; in 1992 the project had so far cost £1.2 billion.

Box 6.9 *A34 Newbury Bypass: 1993–99*

The A34 is the third most important north–south road in the UK. Starting at Southampton, it follows a more-or-less direct line up through the south and midlands of England and terminates in Manchester.

The town of Newbury in Berkshire sits astride the road and has been a traffic bottleneck since the late 1970s when stretches of the road either side of the town caused it to become popular.

In 1989 a feasibility study was conducted with a view to building a bypass. A public inquiry for the venture was commissioned in 1993; and despite a great deal of local opposition, and protests by environmental lobbies and other vested interests, the project was given the go-ahead in 1995. The value of the contract was £82 million.

The project was completed and the road opened in September 1998 at a cost of £103 million. Shortly after it opened, the surface began to break up; and in July 1999 the road was closed for five months while it was re-laid.

The contractors (the venturers) were Balfour Beatty. Publicly, the company acknowledged its error and put the matter right free of charge. However, it subsequently became apparent that the margins on which the company was working were so tight that work had indeed had to be carried out during adverse weather conditions that were known to be potentially damaging to the facility when it was finally opened. Moreover, the hidden and derived costs of this venture, in terms of losses and delays sustained by people now having to use the original facility, have never been calculated.

Box 6.10   *The privatisation of rail services*

When Britain's rail services were entrusted to private bidders, each franchise awarded came up with positive proposals for the future of the services. Promises of new trains and new services helped convince those who doubted the wisdom of the venture that there was nothing really to worry about. In practice, few of these promises have been delivered.

- National Express were awarded the Gatwick Express franchise in 1992. It promised a fleet of new trains by April 1999. There is no prospect of these trains being in public use before the end of the year 2000.
- Connex was awarded the south-eastern and south-central commuter route franchises also in 1992. It promised 16 new trains on the south-eastern franchise by April 1999. By the year 2000 no new trains had been delivered.

The overwhelming problem that the railway privatisation faced was that the only genuinely viable company was Railtrack plc; and this viability was based on the asset values of the land on which the railway lines and stations were built. The service franchises require extremely high levels of investment, of an order that the franchisees were neither asked for, nor were required to make.

In the year 2000, therefore, the UK government finds itself in a cleft stick. If it were to cancel the franchises, it would have nobody to run the services. If it were to take the services back into public ownership, the share values of the franchise holders would rise to politically unacceptable levels, and the only beneficiaries would be the shareholders in the franchise companies. This is quite apart from the residual political damage that would occur.

OTHER MEASURES

As stated above, people and organisations sometimes go into investment ventures where finance is not the primary or overwhelming drive. Other goals needing evaluation are:

- *Prestige*: In order to measure this for success or failure, the extent and nature of prestige achieved, and in whose eyes, needs to be capable of assessment.

- *Reputation*: Similarly, those seeking to acquire reputation as the result of involvement need to be able to pinpoint the desired reputation and the extent to which this was achieved (see box 6.11).
- *Association*: Again, at the outset, it is essential to define the nature of the desired association and the extent to which this was achieved. Matters of reputation, image and prestige are normally present. So too are matters of dominance and dependence, and this requires to be assessed at the outset also.

Box 6.11   *Use of Madonna and Michael Jackson in soft drinks advertising*

Madonna and Michael Jackson were both hired in 1991 to give an additional boost to the image and reputation of the Coca-Cola and PepsiCo soft drinks companies. The purpose was to generate additional sales, market share, and brand loyalty on the back of 'a young wild image'; and because of their reputation, lifestyle, profile and appearance, these two stars were ideally placed to provide it.

However, in the following months, both Madonna and Michael Jackson crossed the boundary from wild and glamorous to wild and unacceptable. A promotional film made by Madonna was cited as blasphemous by the Catholic Church, while Michael Jackson became embroiled in a child abuse scandal.

The people at whom the campaigns were targeted expressed complete indifference to the alleged scandals surrounding the two stars. However, those with responsibility for the venture at Coca-Cola and PepsiCo corporate headquarters took fright. They cancelled the campaigns and paid the staff off.

CONCLUSIONS

The measurement of investment performance is complex. It requires a high level of contextual knowledge and understanding as well as the capability to choose the right financial quantitative and qualitative measures. It also means ensuring that the right points of inquiry are identified and addressed; and this takes place in the context indicated and varies between ventures. From this, those responsible are able to identify what contributes to successful, effective and profitable venture performance; and what contributes to failure. They can also pinpoint:

- the range of activities that contribute to effective, successful and profitable performance, the extent and nature of that contribution, and the effects of each upon the others;
- those activities that do not make any direct contribution to performance;
- those activities that detract from successful and effective venture performance; that damage or destroy it; that dilute its effectiveness;
- those parts of ventures that serve as diversions from purpose; those parts of ventures that cause blockages and barriers to progress;
- the necessary instruments for the management of crises and emergencies when these become apparent;
- appropriate and effective measures of performance set in the particular context.

Only by measuring and assessing all aspects of venture performance, and relating these to the broader context in which activities take place, can actual success and failure be judged. This enables statements such as 'this was pretty successful', or 'that was a total disaster' to be further quantified and examined, and reasons found. It indicates areas where lessons can be learned and improvements made for the future. Only in those simple cases can any linear measurement of investment performance be made; and even these are subject to risk. In more complex ventures, the assessment and management of risk is a key part of the process of conducting successful ventures and measuring their performance.

7 Risk and Investment

INTRODUCTION

The management of risks in investment is one area in which there has been a market upturn in activity on the part of both investors and venturers. Evidence quoted by Dixon (1994) stated that: 'only 37% of the firms sampled analysed risk. When it is remembered that the sample was 150 firms within the bracket of the 300 largest quoted companies in the UK, it can be appreciated for the majority of businesses, risk is hardly assessed, if at all.'

However, writing in *Business Consultancy* in October 1998, Anderson states that:

'as a result of economic changes, there has been an increased emphasis on risk management. This increased emphasis is supported by two separate surveys carried out by Price Waterhouse Coopers in 1998. For example, in a survey of 300 of the largest European companies, 86% of international boards or audited committees had formally reviewed the companies' risk management in the last twelve months. In a separate survey of middle market companies – businesses with a turnover of between £5 million to £200 million – 80% believed risk management to be fundamental to success' (see box 7.1).

It is usual to draw the distinction between risk and uncertainty. Risk is inherent in a situation that is partially, but not fully, known or understood, and therefore can be insured against; while in the unknown there is no point of reference, and therefore this cannot be insured against.

It is clear that those who fail to assess or analyse risk do so from a largely subjective point of view. This may be for the following reasons:

- the feeling that endless assessment of risk leads to inertia, lack of progress and missed opportunities;
- a lack of will to look at the downside of what is superficially a very strong or attractive proposal;
- a lack of understanding of the processes of risk assessment;

- external pressure to produce something quickly rather than doing the job in the correct way.

Attention to risk assessment need not take long, provided that the process is clearly understood. Moreover, it is a short behavioural step from failing to recognise the risks involved to assuming that there are no risks and that therefore the venture will be successful. The following main points need to be addressed.

Box 7.1 *'The greater the risk, the greater the reward'*

It should be apparent by now that this statement is rubbish!! Rewards are gained by the careful assessment of ventures and proposals, not by rushing headlong into them assuming that guesswork, intuition – even projections and forecasts – will automatically be satisfied.

The point is not necessarily helped however, when high-profile entrepreneurs draw attention to their 'high risk' strategies. For example, Richard Branson has described his forays into both airlines and railways as constituting high-risk strategies. This would indeed be the case if all of the other steps indicated so far in the pages of this book had not been taken. However, when going into airlines, Branson took every step possible to ensure that he was surrounded with the required expertise, technology, capital equipment and access to facilities that would give the venture the best possible chance of success. Similarly, when venturing into the railway industry, he took great care to surround himself with the necessary expertise, technology and access to facilities that would give the greatest possible chance of success. The company has initially concentrated on those factors inside its control – attention to passenger care; refurbishment of trains; quality of service; and access to facilities. It has also involved recognising those factors outside the control of the venture – the quality of the railway permanent way, signalling, relations with Railtrack – in order that the overall provision can be substantially improved. Branson has also concentrated, alongside this, on ensuring that the Virgin brand continues to be built and enhanced through advertising and marketing campaigns, and drawing attention to the continued success of other projects and ventures.

Source: *The Money Programme Lecture*, BBC, 12 December 1998.

COMPONENTS OF RISK ASSESSMENT

The following components of risk assessment need to be established.

- *Social, political and economic issues*: the factors over which the venturers have no control.
- *The constitution of the organisations involved in the venture*: their directorates, executives and management, with particular reference to style, attitude and capability.
- *The culture of the organisations involved*: their attitudes to investments and ventures; attitudes to risk; and including evidence of the energy, resources and finance levels with which they are prepared to back their judgement.
- *Monitoring, evaluation and projection processes*: these cover

  Identification of the best, medium and worst outcomes of the venture as a whole, and of the component parts and steps along the way;
  Identification and analysis of any critical path or critical incidents;
  Relative ability to extricate oneself from the situation (or not) and the consequences of this;
  Assessment of the full range of costs and charges that have to be borne in pursuit of the venture.

- *Availability of, and access to, the desired volume and quality of information*: and if this is not readily available, the costs and charges involved in gaining access. It is essential that this is considered from the point of view of gathering:

  Primary information – volumes and quality of information gathered by the venturers in support of the venture;
  Secondary information – information available from other sources, and gathered for other purposes, which may nevertheless be of some use to the particular venture in question.

- *Time factors*: especially where time pressures are coming from, and the consequences of not meeting deadlines.
- *Sectoral trends*: whether growing or declining, either in size or prosperity, and whether this is likely to continue. This also means assessing those factors that are affecting the sector at present; and whether these are likely to affect it in the future; and could possibly, even remotely, affect it at some point.
- *Substitutes*: whether a particular venture may encourage the invention and production of substitute and alternative products and services.
- *Degree of market captivity*: the extent to which the market is captive or fluid, and the reasons for this; the effects on this of the particular venture.

- *Strategic aspects*: relative to the position of the different parties in their own sectors; their preferred direction; their size; the extent to which they are able to dominate or take control of their own future; the extent to which they are market-led, supply-led, or demand-driven; the balance of proactive, steady-state, responsive and crisis activities.
- *Operational effectiveness*: of all those concerned in the venture, especially in relation to the establishment of precise policies, goals and objectives over the short, medium and long term.
- *Identification of the critical requirements of the success of the activities*: this is truly dependent upon the executive capabilities and influence of those involved. Above all, this part of the process requires a full consideration of the questions: 'What can possibly go wrong?' and 'What is the single most important factor to success?'.
- *Causes and effects*: the identification of those parts of the venture where successful implementation of one aspect is dependent upon specific outcomes from others.
- *Early warning systems*: so that problems, crises and dramas from whatever source can be noted early and remedial action taken.

Addressing these points means that an initial analysis of the nature, extent and prevalence of elements of risk, both present and potential, can be undertaken.

RISK ANALYSIS

In general, the outcome of investments is always affected by those forces outside the control of those involved in the venture. Changes in public taste, consumer demand, interest rates and currency values all have effects that can only partly be predicted.

In addition to this, there are conditions unique to the parties involved that have to be assessed and analysed:

- workforce capacity and potential
- technological capacity and potential
- market capacity and potential; and the expertise necessary to fulfil this potential
- particular ways of working
- the location of executive power, authority and influence
- key characters, functions and expertise
- local factors
- aspects of difficulty, value, frequency, importance and presentation;
- the quality and effectiveness of decision-making processes.

Effective analysis of risk requires that each party to the venture takes, as far as possible, a rational approach to each of these aspects so that an initial assessment can be made of whether the capacity to sustain the particular initiative is present. It is thus that an accurate or informed assessment of the risks involved in any venture is produced in advance. This does not mean that risks are not taken, but rather that an informed judgement has been made before going on to the next stage. If this is done, a truer range of outcomes can be assessed; more accurate contingency plans can be drawn up; and any future issues can be evaluated from a position of relative strength and certainty.

SPREADING THE RISK

One approach to the management of risk is to spread the investment in such a way so as to ensure that the potential for substantial losses is minimised. For example, an ice cream manufacturer is heavily dependent upon the weather for its products to be attractive. It may expect the greatest demand for its products during the summer. It may experience a sudden upsurge in demand for its products if there is a sudden hot spell either in the spring or the autumn; and a downturn for its products if the weather is cold or wet during the summer.

The risk inherent in such a venture can be spread by diversifying into the manufacture of soup. However, the company would then become a new player in a territory that is already well established and dominated by familiar brands. Spreading the risk therefore has consequences afresh: while the initial premise may be 'rational' for entering into the soup industry, the true extent of investment necessary to gain familiarisation, commercialisation and profitable returns may make the venture unrealistic; and so fresh approaches would have to be sought.

The financial services industry spreads personal and corporate investments among a mix of: government stocks (which bring a low, though guaranteed, rate of return); deposit accounts (which bring better, though still low and guaranteed, rates of return); stocks and shares (which may fluctuate wildly in the short term); and currencies (which may also fluctuate wildly in the short term). However, by adopting this approach, the risk of substantial losses, and the consequent loss of client confidence, can be minimised. In order to be fully successful however, those making the investments need to have understood in advance the extent and nature of the risks involved in each of the sectors – it is not enough simply to apportion parts of the total investment in the hope that things 'will not be too bad' (see box 7.2).

Box 7.2 *Manchester United Football Club*

In October 1998 Manchester United Football Club announced its intention of opening 150 retail outlets world-wide. The stated intention was to capitalise on the recent history of football success that the club had enjoyed, and the consequent upturn in world interest.

The risk inherent in such a venture stemmed from the fact that, other than its own (admittedly substantial) retail outlet at its Old Trafford ground, the company had no experience in the global retail sector. Accordingly, the venture was projected on the sheer strength of the brand name alone. It was also not clear whether extensive interest in watching the games on satellite television across the world would translate into sales of merchandise at levels that would make this a successful and profitable venture. The venture was proposed at a time when, in the UK and Europe, those interested in football were nevertheless beginning seriously to question whether or not the merchandise was worth acquiring. This was exacerbated when a report produced in October 1999 on behalf of the UK Football Association and its leading clubs stated that 'supporters would have to pay increasing prices for an evermore rapidly changing range of merchandise in order to maintain identity with the clubs'.

RISK AND SENSITIVITY

The degree of sensitivity of a particular venture or proposal can be calculated once the initial projections have been completed. This is carried out in one of three ways.

- A single factor is selected at random and different projections placed upon it; the effect of changes to this single factor can then be calculated.
- Two or more factors are selected at random and their projections recalculated; and from this, calculations of the effects of these on the rest of the venture can be carried out.
- All factors are subject to random recalculation. This last is designed to ensure that the extent of lack of certainty or control in the venture is at least addressed.

Beyond that, analysing the sensitivity of different aspects of the venture enables assessment to be made of the overall relative strength or weakness of the venture, and of any single factor on which its successful outcome depends.

It is also possible to develop this a stage further by selecting a purely random value (either based on random numbers or random selection by computer programme) for each different element and to calculate the effect of random occurrences upon the totality of the venture. This is likely to throw up the wildly unlikely and fantastic suggestions (e.g. what would be the effect on the venture of the UK currency halving/doubling in value in the next six months?). However again, it encourages the consideration of the venture from as broad a perspective as possible. Moreover, some of the random factors will be much closer to potential or reality than this example.

'WHAT IF?' APPROACHES

It is also useful to extrapolate what might or might not happen in particular situations. The 'What if?' approach can be used in a variety of ways to do this.

- *Events*: for example – what if there is a strike while work is in progress? What if there is an equipment failure? What if one of those involved goes bankrupt? What if one of those involved is taken over?
- *People*: for example – what if one of the key players pulls out or loses confidence? What if there is a change of key personnel along the way?
- *Past history*: for example – what if a 'soft' currency on which we depend halves in value? What if it doubles in value? What if there is a war or revolution in Russia/Thailand/Indonesia/Yugoslavia/Germany/wherever else we are being asked to invest?
- *The unheard of and unthought of*: for example – what if interest rates in the UK are 0.5 per cent/20 per cent/anything in between this time next year or in five years' time? What if the Dollar halves/doubles/quadruples in value?
- *Attractive side shows*: for example – what if oil/construction/cork/linoleum suddenly becomes the thing to invest in for the greatest prospect of short- to medium-term returns? What if our main backer pulls out to take advantage of this in three years' time?
- *The 'totally unthinkable'*: for example – what if there is a technological revolution that enables ships, airlines, houses to be built and fitted out in a week? What if the stock market halves/doubles its index in three months?

It is possible to feed these points and other variations on these themes into computer programs that then extrapolate and project possible outcomes. It is also well worth while having professional discussions along these lines in order to make sure that everyone involved has at least thought of the range of alternative and diverse outcomes possible in a particular venture (see box 7.3).

Box 7.3 *Investment opportunities in Serbia: from 1999 into the twenty-first century*

At the end of the war in Kosovo and the bombing campaign in Serbia in 1999, the United Nations, World Bank and warring protagonists proposed a financial schedule for the rebuilding of the Serbian infrastructure that had been damaged or destroyed by the military action.

Superficially, the opportunities were apparent to everyone. Consequently, there was a great rush of interest on the part of management consultants, construction, civil engineering and other capital project based companies to draw upon the investment made available by the United Nations and World Bank. In particular, many of these companies came from USA, UK and other countries within the European Union – those countries that had been most heavily involved in the bombing campaigns against Serbia. Here, it seemed, was an opportunity to benefit from the war.

The risks involved were less apparent, and only when ventures began to be drawn up as proposals for action did they become clear. Matters that those with the greatest enthusiasm for reconstruction work had largely ignored were as follows.

- The resentment of the Serb government and Serb people over having their facilities rebuilt at great cost to themselves by agents of the warring powers.
- The inability to secure local cooperation without making substantial payments into community funds.
- The inability to insure against further civil unrest or political upheaval.
- The strength of the army as the dominant force in Serb and greater Yugoslavian politics.
- Logistical problems caused by the fact that much of the road and rail infrastructure had been destroyed in the fighting.

DURATION

Duration has to be approached from all points of view as follows.

- The duration of the commitment required on the part of all those involved, whether finance and backing, expertise, resources, equipment and technology.
- The duration of the venture itself over the period of initial commitment to delivery of the final product, service or project; and the delivery of the financial returns.
- The duration of the useful life of the finished or completed venture.
- The duration of the value of the venture to the particular markets, customers, clients and end-users concerned.

Duration has also to be considered from the point of view of:

- possible changes in political, economic and social circumstances, priorities, pressures and expectations over the lifespan of the venture; this is of especial importance when assessing long-term capital project work;
- the extent to which resources committed over a long period of time can be managed effectively; it is essential, where this is the case, that staging posts and punctuation marks are established. When dealing with personal clients and investors, the financial services industry requires that independent financial advisers and investment houses have at least an annual meeting with their clients;
- the durability of technology, expertise and other non-financial resources over the period of the venture;
- the duration of relationships over the period of the venture; and the consequence of changes in these. Those who invest in supply side normally look for a multiplicity of providers (sometimes called multi-sourcing) as a way round this; while there are ever-greater commercial pressures on acknowledged long-term investments such as in drug and pharmaceutical research to gain product acceptability and commercialisation as quickly as possible.

PAYBACK AND RETURNS

Assuming that everyone has come into the particular situation with clear ideas of the returns desired and required, the likelihood of these being achieved has to be assessed. These then need to be re-appraised using 'What if?' and other approaches indicated above. In particular, the likelihood and consequences of payback periods being extended, or payments being reduced, need full evaluation (see box 7.4).

Box 7.4   *The payback method*

Payback is undoubtedly the most popular method of analysis of risk in practice and this is as true for large firms as for small. However, the fact that only 32 per cent of firms used payback as a primary risk evaluation method and that 90 per cent of firms which used more than one method of analysis used payback as one of those methods, strongly suggests that payback is often seen as a back-up method for more sophisticated and theoretically superior techniques. This back-up value is enhanced by the fact that payback is a method whose whole purpose is often quoted (rightly or wrongly) as being to ensure against the presence of risk in an undertaking. Analysed industry by industry, payback is almost universally popular – 84 per cent of capital goods firms and 94 per cent of consumer durables firms use payback as an evaluation technique.

The popularity of the payback technique is due mostly to the fact that it is easy to understand and simple to use. Typifying those who use the technique was the comment: 'it is simple, quick to produce and readily understood particularly by non-financial and over extended management'.'

Source: R. Dixon, *Investment Appraisal: A Guide for Managers*, Kogan Page, 1994.

The other main way of using the payback method to manage risk is to shorten the payback period. This especially becomes important where conditions are uncertain, because venturers seek to gain their returns on one particular stage of the process, before committing funds, technology, expertise or other resources to the next part.

SIZE, SCOPE AND SCALE OF MARKETS

Reference was made above to the duration of markets. The nature of the market also needs full evaluation. This is because any new venture, whether into an existing and familiar situation, or something that is completely new, has consequences for the rest of the operations. The venture may simply add to the choice and the variety available to customers, clients, consumers and end-users. At the other extreme, it may seriously destabilise the market. This is especially the case where the venture becomes a victim of its own success.

What usually happens is that there is an initial demand for its outputs that simply cannot be satisfied. This, in turn, leads to frustration, loss of confidence and ultimately rejection – and therefore long-term failure of the venture.

Customer, Consumer, Client and End-User Behaviour and Consequences

Ventures can be designed and put together based on general assessment of these elements; or greatly detailed approaches may be taken. Neither is a guarantee of success. A clear understanding of the position of the venture in terms of customer, client, consumer and end-user priority importance, value, known and perceived acceptability is essential, however. This has to be seen in the context of the relative transience, faddishness and overall subjectivity of the behaviour of these groups. It has also to be seen in terms of known and perceived mutuality of interest, confidence and expectations. This applies in equal measure to investment in capital projects and professional ventures, as to those that are eventually to be used by individuals.

Consequences of Success

The consequences of success are rarely evaluated. However, if a venture succeeds beyond everyone's wildest dreams then it is apparent that (*a*) the forecasting and projections were inadequate; (*b*) there will be effects of this success on other activities currently being pursued.

For organisations with limited resources, the latter point is serious because they then have to make choices about where to concentrate their efforts both at present and in future – whether to go with the direction indicated by the current venture, or stick to hitherto successful work elsewhere. So when this occurs, evaluation of prospects for the future and the nature of success of the current venture must take place.

A simple approach to this is to re-evaluate all activities as:

- those that attract interest, investment and funds
- those that attract reputation and confidence
- those that make money

	and

- those that do not attract interest, investment, funds
- those that dilute, or cause loss of, reputation and confidence
- those that lose money.

And from this, to establish a basis for analysing, judging and evaluating the outcomes of such re-appraisal.

This at least helps to put the current venture in perspective and to ensure that people (*a*) do not get carried away with the current success; (*b*) begin to understand why it is being judged a success; (*c*) consider whether the basis of this judgement is sustainable in the future.

Success may also lead to levels of expectation for the future that are not possible to sustain without extensive further investment. This occurs especially when investment in pharmaceutical or information technology research is known, believed or perceived to be successful and there is a consequent sudden upsurge in demand for the end product.

Consequences of Failure

In the same way, failure needs recognition and assessment. Organisations and their managers are not good at this (see box 7.5).

Box 7.5 *Lockheed*

The Lockheed Corporation of America used to be a major independent aircraft manufacturer and defence contractor. The following incidents occurred to the company during the latter years of its independent life.

- It produced the *Electra* turbo-prop airliner, several years too late, and at a time when more advanced players in the industry (especially Boeing) were starting to mass produce jet airliners.
- The *Cheyenne* helicopter, designed for both military and civil aviation purposes, was more bulky, cumbersome and expensive to operate than its rivals, and also could not carry the same volumes of people or equipment.
- The *Galaxy* military transport airliner was too large for any airport that could not take jumbo jets.
- The *F104 Starfighter*, designed as an all-pupose single-seater military machine for the Cold War, was flawed in design and technology.
- The *Tristar* airbus also suffered design faults and lateness of delivery. In this case, the problem was compounded by the fact that Lockheed contracted with Rolls-Royce to supply engines for the plane; and these could not be supplied either at an acceptable quality or at a reasonable price.

Reviewing the period (1963–81) over which these disasters took place, a former senior manager of the company said: 'We've asked ourselves what we did wrong, and we concluded that there really wasn't anything'.

Investment failures normally result in:

- denial
- calls for further backing to mitigate losses incurred
- demands for government/EU/UN/NATO assistance
- profits/losses warnings in the media
- resort to soundbites and financial sector blandness (see box 7.6).
- blame and infighting among partners in the venture.

Box 7.6   *Excuses for failure*

The failure of investment ventures is normally put down to one or more of the following, at least at corporate level.

- Fluctuations in interest rates, inflation, retail prices index, currency values and other economic factors that 'simply could not be predicted or foreseen'.
- Currency collapses or surges making the venture either too expensive to complete on the part of the investor; or too expensive to take delivery of on the part of the venturer.
- Turbulence in the global economy.
- Changes in consumer demand and confidence caused by, so it is stated, 'unfair trading practices on the part of Japanese/Korean/ Taiwanese/ Mongolian/South African companies (as if these factors have not been known for generations).
- The promulgation of news media stories about perceived unfair and unethical trading practices. The most popular of these still continues to be the practice of market flooding and product dumping on the part of Far Eastern companies of their products and services in Western Europe and North America. Again, this practice has been going on for at least thirty years; and again, if the products were no good, people would not buy them.
- Resorting to public relations coaching: in which the failure of investments is presented in such impersonal ways as: 'projected synergies did not take place'; 'productivitisation failed to occur'; 'economies of scale were not achieved'.

Source: *The Times*, 14 September 1999 (all examples).

Given that everyone went into the venture with their own clear aims and objectives, and understanding the purposes of the others involved, there is a most detailed structure on which a full analysis of failure can be carried out.

The basis for this structure is to return to the aims and objectives agreed. Following on from that, the first step is to admit the possibility of failure. The second is to recognise that historically, either failure or shortage of full success occurs on nearly 90 per cent of occasions (Industrial Society, 1993). The third step is to recognise the sheer folly of guessing at causes, effects and solutions when failure becomes apparent (see box 7.7).

Box 7.7 *Failure and the football industry*

When Bobby Robson was appointed manager of Newcastle United Football Club in September 1999, the club had spent nearly £200 million on its ground and facilities, and on player transfers. Other than promotion into the UK Premier Football League, the club had won nothing; though it had appeared in two FA Cup Finals.

Robson was the club's fourth manager in five years. As each of the previous managers had been appointed, they were able to spend additional money investing in new players; and this was often with little regard to the capabilities or asset value of the players that they had inherited from the previous incumbent. The problem had therefore been managed, until the date of Robson's appointment, as follows:

• It was assumed that if enough money was thrown at the problem (whatever that was – the problem was never clearly defined), everything would 'come right' in the end;
• Insufficient time was given for the assets purchased with all this money to work or become successful;
• Inappropriate appointments and player purchases were made;
• Assumptions were made about two of the managers that, because they had been successful in the past, they would be successful in the future.

No proper analysis or evaluation was carried out. Nobody sought to do anything about the problem, other than to respond to powerful, influential and dominant personalities by giving them as much money as they wanted, to spend as they saw fit, without reference to purpose, aims, objectives or definition of the purpose of investment, or returns on that investment.

This then forms a full operational basis on which effective review can take place. If it has been reinforced by a formalised system of regular 'punctuation mark' reviews and monitoring of activities during the period of the venture, then this, in any case, becomes easier. It also helps to develop the quality of relationship that is essential if full confidence in the venture is to be maintained and developed.

CRISES

If forecasting, prediction and extrapolation were perfect techniques, then there would never be any crises anywhere, but in reality the prospect of crises and emergencies can never be avoided entirely. However, it is possible to take steps to assess where they are likely to occur, why, and whether this is as the result of factors inside or outside the control of those involved. These factors are itemised using the various techniques illustrated, and the results evaluated. Each item then needs further assessment from the extreme points of view so that the 'unthinkable' is indeed considered.

A key feature of the management of investor relationships is the agreement and establishment of early warning systems so that any problem is recognised early and nipped in the bud. Crises are then limited to being the result of the genuinely unforeseen, and to what the insurance industry calls 'acts of God' (e.g. earthquakes, floods and so on) (see box 7.8).

Box 7.8   *Private prisons*

In the early 1990s the UK government attracted private investment into the Prison Service. The stated aim was to reduce the charges on the public purse by putting some of the less extreme and overtly easily managed niches in the service out to contract. By paying a fee to the investor, this would cost less than if the particular parts of the service remained in the public sector.

The earliest private contractor to invest in the Prison Service was Group 4-Securitas. During the first week of its activities, three 'low risk' prisoners absconded from a Group 4 van while they were being taken to court to hear the charges against them. The staff had not been trained to lock the doors of the van, neither had anyone in the company thought it important enough to establish procedures to make sure that this was indeed carried out.

This became:

(1) *A political crisis*: because it called instantly into question the main problems inherent in moving public services away from those sectors where public service professionals were used to dealing with particular groups of people;
(2) *A media crisis*: because the story caused all sorts of different investigations into the nature, quality and content of the venture; and the contracted arrangements that supported it;
(3) *A cash crisis*: because the arrangements for paying for the management of crises, and in particular the additional costs incurred by the contractor as a result of this and other 'unforeseen' circumstances, had not been fully worked out.

The following have also subsequently become apparent.

• The calculations upon which it was decided that Prison Service management would be more cost effective if private contractors were drawn into the service were flawed. This especially hinged on the writing down of public assets as if they were bought and paid for at current values (rather than when they were actually bought and paid for, which in many cases was anything up to 100 years previously).
• There was nothing to stop the private contractor withdrawing at a moment's notice from the venture; and were this to happen, the clients of the venturer would instantly become the responsibility of the public sector.
• The public facilities sold or leased to the venturer have, because of their often prime site locations, a potential economic rent and asset value far in excess of that which is written into the contract. Those involved in ventures such as these therefore have clear opportunity to acquire sites for development at prices that, from their point of view, are extremely good value.

It follows from this that all ventures need contingency funds in order to cope with wholly or partly unforeseen circumstances; and this applies to all parties to the venture. It is not possible to predict events absolutely, thus their true extent and impact is never fully apparent until they do occur or after they have occurred. So their potential effects have to be recognised and underwritten.

CONCLUSIONS

The approach outlined in this chapter is designed to ensure that those involved in ventures understand the full range of possible outcomes. Each of the factors indicated needs full expert and professional evaluation in the particular situation, and in terms of the venture in question. If this evaluation is needed quickly, then risk assessment procedures and approaches need to be built in, so that this can be done properly. The alternative is simply to cut corners, effectively to gamble with the resources and future of those involved in the venture.

It is also clear that the management of risk is not simply concerned with having access to duplicate expertise, technology, equipment, resources or supplies. It is not enough simply to throw financial resources at problems. It is not enough to engage bureaucratic mechanisms, techniques and processes on their own because these tend to become slow and cumbersome and lead to lost opportunities. Neither is it enough to feed a set of data and variables – however comprehensive – into a computer programme and then to take the outputs of the machine as absolute fact. Whichever approach is taken must produce information that is capable of being used to support and inform the judgement of those with responsibility for taking investment decisions.

Finally, the establishment of a fully comprehensive process of assessing risk enables all those involved in the venture to build up their expertise in operating in the particular environment. This can then be used to develop their own approaches so that they become expert, rather than intuitive (i.e. using guesswork), in the particular area.

8 Managing Investor Relations

INTRODUCTION

The management and development of relationships between those involved is another part of the whole process that is often neglected. It is either assumed that those involved will be able to work together in harmony for the duration of the venture; or else it is assumed that the benefits that are planned to accrue will indeed come about and that this will transcend any personal or professional differences that are otherwise apparent (see box 8.1).

Box 8.1 *London Underground link to Heathrow Terminal 4*

The contract for this work was awarded to Balfour Beatty, the UK civil engineering company. Balfour Beatty, in turn, appointed Hangartner GmbH of Vienna, Austria, as tunnelling consultants to oversee the structure of the venture, and to propose different approaches for the successful completion of the project.

The project was duly completed and handed over to London Transport.

Shortly after its opening, the tunnel collapsed. An inquiry was held and the conclusion was that insufficient attention had been paid to the durability of the finished project, and that, especially, the tunnel lining had not been properly anchored. Following further scrutiny of the contract documentation, Balfour Beatty were prosecuted. They denied liability, stating that they were working to the prescription and standards proposed by Hangartner.

Hangartner denied this. They produced contract specifications and their proposals, demonstrating that they had indeed requested specific attention to the stability of the tunnel lining. The case proceeded to litigation, and the court found against Balfour Beatty. The company was fined £1.2 million.

Explaining itself after the verdict, the company cited misunderstandings between themselves and Hangartner caused by language barriers and difficulties, misunderstandings of the costings, and the physical distance that existed between the location of the contract and Vienna.

151

MANAGEMENT PROCESSES IN INVESTMENT RELATIONS

Effective management of the process must cover the following.

- *Management of the financial aspects of the venture*: based on accurate, high-quality information available to, and understood by, everyone involved.
- *Management of the work and tasks inherent in the venture itself*: including the establishment and acceptance of work methods, timescales, resource gathering, problem-solving and maintenance functions.
- *Management of the personal and professional aspects*: including identifying and addressing barriers to understanding and progress; and identifying and using formats that develop the personal aspect of the relationships.
- *Managing communications*: between the different parties to the venture, with especial reference to cultural and language difficulties; to identify potential conflicts early, and to propose ways in which these are managed effectively.
- *Attention to individuals*: making constructive use of talents and expertise of all those involved; and ensuring that individual contributions transcend any differences in financial balance of the venture.
- *Management style*: the creation and adoption of a style that is both positive and dynamic, and also suitable to the management needs of the venture; adopting a style that transcends cultural differences and expectations where necessary.
- *Maintenance and development management*: ensuring that administration and support services are designed for, and suitable for, the needs of the venture.
- *Establishment of common aims and objectives*: understood, valued and accepted by all those involved.
- *Policy, cohesion and shared values*: standards of attitude, behaviour and performance that all those involved can agree to work to, and in which they have confidence and belief.
- *Venture spirit*: akin to team spirit, the development of a positive commitment, high levels of motivation, positive identity, and loyalty to the venture, the tasks in hand, and to each other. While the positive contribution of this is not always fully realised or evaluated, the negative effects – infighting and jockeying for position, sub-grouping and lobbying – are always destructive.
- *Leadership and direction*: this is referred to above; leadership style must again transcend any cultural or perceptual differences if the venture is to succeed fully.
- *Management of responsibility and accountability*: the boundaries for this are established; the remit of those involved in the venture is defined and

accepted by all those involved; organisational and professional responsibilities are noted.

Clearly, the mix of this varies between ventures. In the management of a
deposit account or personal investment schemes, for example, ultimate
responsibility for the effectiveness of the process lies with the depositor.
Responsibility for the performance of the deposit, on the other hand, rests
with the bank or finance house. If the depositor does not like the management style, attitudes or values that are exhibited by the finance house, they
either put up with this, or else move their funds elsewhere.

For long-term, complex, commercial and public service ventures, the
process is more complex, and the consequences of ineffective relations or
loss of confidence cannot be resolved simply by seeking to remove oneself
from the venture. So it is important that each of the elements indicated
above is addressed fully once the commitment to invest has been made.

The Parties in Investment Appraisal

The main parties are:

- venturers, inventors, proposers of ideas, those with project proposals;
- backers (investors), those with resources, finance, expertise, technology
  and reputation to bring to a particular venture.

This is the key relationship. It has to be assessed and established from
each of the above points in the process. It then has to be manageable from
the following points of view.

- *Dominance-dependency*: The process indicated above identifies where the
  problems inherent in any dominance–dependency aspect of the relationship may occur; and these can then be managed. Where it is clear that
  someone is going to dominate the relationship, everyone involved should
  at least understand the fact; and those dependent on the relationship can
  assess their own position in the light of this enquiry.
- *Returns required*: Again, the establishment of an effective management
  process is much more likely to bring out into the open the feasibility of
  desired or required levels of return.
- *Human contact*: This especially refers to the frequency and agenda of
  regular formalised meetings to monitor and review progress. Meeting
  structures are also required for crises and emergencies. Formats for
  contacts between the different parties, and those not directly involved
  in the venture, also need to be established.
- *Professional contract arrangements*, which formalise the nature of the
  relationship and include precise statements of responsibilities, liabilities,

profit cost and loss sharing, and contingency and crisis management funds (see box 8.2).

- *Duration*: in which it needs to be recognised that individuals representing organisations involved in long-term ventures are likely to change over periods of time and that a good professional relationship may be diluted by subsequent professional or personality clashes.

Box 8.2 *Professional contracts*

There are two archetypes of this.

- *The complementary or integrated*: in which the contracts for the venture are designed from an open and positive point of view. This sounds admirable. In practice, however, it only works when there is full openness of information and full confidence in the individuals involved. It requires all parties to nominate precisely the areas of responsibility, liability, profit, cost and loss that they will bear in the event of any of these elements arising. Specific conditions imposed on any party are stated.
- *The adversarial or distributive*: in which the contract is formed on the basis that the venture will come to fruition as stated at the outset. Any problems that arise along the way are settled by negotiation, bargaining and, if this does not work, by litigation. This also includes reference to any specific conditions. Unforeseen circumstances normally become the subject of claim and counterclaim. This form of contract is superficially attractive to public service ventures, defence contracting, building, construction, civil and other engineering ventures for the simple reason that all those involved are used to dealing with these ventures in this way. However, it is an extremely expensive way of proceeding; and the main output from a relationship point of view is that there is no mutuality of trust, loyalty, or understanding.

Both approaches are legally binding. So also are any approaches that try to take a line in between the two extremes. Equivalent forms of contract also exist in personal investment ventures, in which the parties are the individual, their personal investment adviser or independent financial adviser, and the company or institution with which the funds are invested. The form of contract must be presented to the individual investor by whoever is advising them or accepting their funds for investment.

Other Parties

The other parties involved in a relationship are the other stakeholders identified. Relations with these have also to be managed.

It is useful to draw a diagrammatic representation of these interests (see Figure 8.1).

In general therefore, the effective management of investment relations has to consider the following.

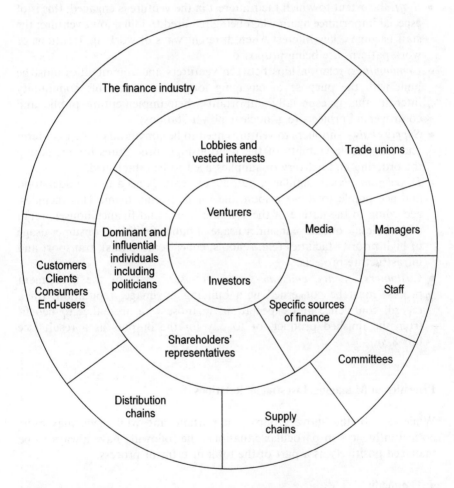

Notes
The key relationship is at the centre; the greatest other influences are in the middle circle.
The potential effects of those in the outer circle must not be underestimated. The extent, prevalence and influence of all groups must be assessed.

Figure 8.1   *Investment relations*

- *The finance industry*: from the point of view of prevailing norms and expectations; the ways in which its business is conducted; the effect of regulators.
- *Trade unions*: the extent and prevalence of their influence, and their potential for affecting the outcome of particular ventures.
- *Managers*: their ability to work together, across cultures and organisational boundaries where necessary; their own personal aims and objectives for career development.
- *Staff*: the extent to which their interest in the venture is engaged; this is of especial importance again when being required to join a joint venture; the staff become a key interest when different ways of working, locations or work patterns are being proposed.
- *Communities*: relationships between venturers and communities must be built with the purpose of engaging long-term sustainable community interest; this is especially important when implementing public and controversial projects (e.g. nuclear power stations).
- *Supply chains*: suppliers to ventures need to be convinced of the long-term and sustainable viability of the relationships; procedures for regulating the ordering and delivery of supplies need to be established.
- *Distribution chains*: similarly, outputs of ventures need to be understood and acceptable to those responsible for delivering them. This includes, according to the nature of the venture: banks and finance houses; retail and wholesale outlets; consumer usage of public facilities; consumer usage of high priority facilities (e.g. schools, colleges, hospitals); transport and infrastructure projects.
- *Customers, clients, consumers and end-users*: part of the investment process must be concerned with building up image, reputation, track record, confidence and expectations in those who are either to benefit from the finished product, or to pay for the outputs as a result (see box 8.3).

Priorities in Managing Investment Relations

While each of the above groups is important; and while each may exert critical influences in particular situations, the following have always to be managed positively as a part of the total investment process.

- The media
- Shareholders, backers and their representatives
- Lobbies, pressure groups and vested interests
- Influential individuals including politicians.

These are the groups identified in the middle circle of Figure 8.1.

Box 8.3   *Managing investment relations: examples*

Channel Tunnel

When the project was first commissioned, Eurotunnel were faced with:

- micro-political and vested interest antagonism – in the form of 'the project will ruin the political independence, viability and identity of the UK';
- social – the environmental blight created by the construction and operation of the project had to be assessed and managed;
- economic – people wondered what would happen to their jobs in other parts of the transport and cross-Channel industries when the project became fully operational.

Eurotunnel's approach was to become instantly 'good corporate citizens'. From the outset, the company's facilities were thrown open to groups needing places to meet, and these included: the Women's Institute, the Brownies, the Scouts. The company provided initial and continuing sponsorship for local events such as firework displays, the local carnival, and educational facilities. The company archives were opened to researchers and students. The company engaged in an education programme targeted at primary and secondary schools to engage the understanding, knowledge and support of children (and therefore their families). Finally, the company undertook to use local labour wherever possible, both for the construction, and also for the operation of the finished project.

Railtrack

By contrast, the construction of the railway link to the Channel Tunnel on the UK side of the project ran into all sorts of difficulties. Railtrack plc, the UK national railway owner, and the company responsible for ensuring that the new railway link was delivered, refused to become involved in any public debate on the subject. Spokespeople refused to speak to the press. The company refused to provide speakers for lobbies and vested interest groups. Security and access to the company's offices in Ashford, Kent, were restricted. The company archives remain a matter of confidentiality.

The project was finally started in April 1998. So far, there has been no wide-ranging initiative to manage relationships with those directly affected by the project; neither has the company sought to engage local labour, except where this has become necessary on a short-term basis.

The Media

Most organisations involved in investment projects now understand the need to manage the media and to make it work, where possible to their advantage. The reporting of ventures by the media is subjective and partial and conducted from the point of view of the particular newspaper, journal, radio or television station. These all bring their own versions of events to bear, and their own editorial standpoint, supported where appropriate by expert opinion (not fact); and this expert opinion has normally been sought because it will support the editorial standpoint of the newspaper or broadcaster concerned. It follows from this that the greater the media interest, the greater the propensity for conflicting stories and views on the venture.

This in itself is potentially damaging and destructive. When people are assailed with conflicting views on something, they become uncertain, and this leads to a collective loss of confidence. It is essential therefore that the venture has its own distinctive media standpoint; this will not stop the media from publishing contrasting views on the venture, but it:

(1) Enables a robust, structured and justified rebuttal or commentary to be issued;
(2) Ensures that those responsible for the inception, direction and delivery of the venture have clarified their own position prior to dealing with the media.

So the approach required when managing the media has to be prescribed and directed. If then adverse coverage does come about, the main parties know the steps necessary to remedy this, and to deal elsewhere with specific issues. This is only truly effective if the venture has been appraised from all points of view, rather than being driven by narrow financial or political interests.

Moreover, if there is not a united view concerning the direction and delivery of complex ventures, media coverage will highlight and enhance the divisions that exist. One version of events from one party to a venture is contrasted with versions from other parties. Again, this leads to overall loss of confidence in the direction, credibility and purpose of what is intended (see box 8.4).

Shareholders, Backers and their Representatives

This part of investment relationship management requires especial attention because it is invariably the dominant interest. Those dependent upon loan and other non-share backing (or at the mercy of it) need to satisfy themselves of the following.

- The extent of dominance of the backing interest.
- The integrity of the relationship. This means paying attention to the extent to which the venture is being backed because the investing institution has faith in it; or whether it is the investing institution's particular representative who has faith (see box 8.5).
- The security of the finance involved. This reflects the extent to which the money is genuinely secure for the duration of the venture. Major shareholders put pressure on their representatives to become involved in ventures or to withdraw from them, that may nevertheless run contrary to the views of those responsible for seeing them through to completion. Major shareholders also put pressure on their representatives to become involved in ventures because short-term gains are clearly available; or to withdraw from ventures because short-term gains have now been satisfied.
- Shareholders and their representatives also find attractive investment in those ventures where finance can be insured or underwritten to a greater extent (see box 8.6).
- Their driving interest, which is to gain the desired rates of return for those on whose behalf they are acting. Especially where institutional funds are being used, there is invariably a direct conflict between the demands of investment for long-term assured and secure finance, and the demands for short-term, continued and assured rates of return on the part of investors.

Relationships with shareholders, backers and their representatives are only truly effective if these points are fully understood at the outset. This is in addition to ensuring that mutuality, personal and professional confidence also exists. It is therefore clear that, as each of these elements is present in all investment relationships, no certainty of finance can ever be guaranteed.

Lobbies, Pressure Groups and Vested Interests

These groups exist to an extent in all ventures, and the extent of their knowledge and influence needs to be recognised. They influence all aspects of the venture, and also have different levels of influence among the different parties involved. The following must especially be noted.

- *Residents' associations*: These spring up whenever major investments are being proposed or created in their areas. They have highly subjective and perfectly legitimate concerns. Problems with residents' associations are also exacerbated when they find it impossible to get high quality information about the effects of particular ventures and proposals on the enduring quality of their lives.
- *Environmental lobbies*: These are of especial concern when it is known, believed or perceived that there are to be adverse effects on the

environment as the result of a particular venture. This applies to all capital projects. It also applies to many research ventures (e.g. prospecting for oil is not in itself intrusive or potentially damaging to the environment; however, the creation of oil wells and refinery facilities would be). There are always environmental issues attached to any venture that is concerned with the management, production or disposal of waste, effluent and pollution (see box 8.7).

The key features in the management of environmental lobbies are:

- attention to, and respect for, their concerns;
- extensive and high quality information provision;
- acknowledgement of the environmental effects of particular projects;
- including the management of environmental lobbies as a key concern of the investment process; and this is to be supported, where necessary or desirable, by the engagement of specialists as a consequence of being involved in the particular venture.

If these factors are not addressed as a part of the management of investment relations, then investment relations are managed through the news media and on a confrontational or adversarial basis. This adds to the cost of the venture, both in terms of resources and reputation.

Box 8.4 *The Private Finance Initiative*

The Private Finance Initiative is a major way in which the UK government is seeking to attract private funds and expertise into the creation and management of public facilities and services.

To date, the Home Office (prisons), the Department of Transport, Environment and the Regions (roads, railways and bridges) and the Foreign Office (embassies) have all commissioned projects that are to be conducted under the Private Finance Initiative. In essence, they are to be designed, built, owned and operated by the private sector. Contracting (i.e. investing) companies fund the cost of the project; and, when it is completed, the companies are either paid a lease, or else allowed to recoup their costs through charges to the end-users.

Difficulties with managing the media have been present from the outset; and the problems are clearly illustrated as follows.

Aims and Objectives

The aims and objectives of government were to attract short-term finance and expertise to accelerate and enhance the facilities available for the long-term provision of public facilities.

The aims and objectives of the contractors involved were founded on the capability to attract short-term cash injections; to take up spare capacity in their organisations; and to ensure 'guaranteed' rates of return.

Some harmonisation of aims and objectives is therefore clearly possible. However, the political drive required the demonstration of quick results and, as such, the contracted arrangements, and standards for the delivery of the facilities and services, were never adequately established. Moreover, the cost calculations had to be presented in such a way as to ensure that the attraction of private finance was cost effective, rather than the more expensive way of delivering established services.

However, the problems caused by rushing through the approach, supported only be skewed calculations, in order to demonstrate success for political reasons, soon became apparent. Whenever the contractors faced any unforeseen problems, they simply returned to the government and asked for more money. This was forthcoming. This represented something on which the media could focus, and which became the point of view of investigation and analysis of the projects and services.

It was quickly established that no single set of criteria existed for the evaluation of any of these projects. Especially reporting of the projects by the political interest was limited to blandness. This is exacerbated by the fact that politicians and their officials briefed journalists to the effect that they refused to be pressed or quoted in more detail on such projects. The net result has been to ensure that media interest has been maintained; though not from the point of view of the policy initiative.

Individuals Including Politicians

Over-mighty players exist when they are able to influence the inception, direction or performance of ventures as the result of their own partial interest, expertise, position or personality. Of especial concern is the position when it is known, believed or perceived that a venture has been launched (or cancelled) primarily for the greater glory of one player; or else that it is being used by an influential person to prove a point. This happens from time to time in all areas of investment. It is superficially attractive because particular individuals normally put a great deal of energy into proving themselves right. However, this may store up serious problems further down the line, especially if the particular individual either has a change of mind or else is removed from the venture. It may also lead to serious problems when the rest of the relationship is not clear; and the normal consequence of this is that such individuals are left to their own devices (see box 8.8).

Box 8.5   *Farming in south-eastern England in the 1990s*

Since 1945 a large farming company had enjoyed the full support of its bankers. The relationship between the company and the bank was founded on full professional and personal confidence and mutuality of interest. There were flexible overdraft facilities because it was understood that these were an essential part of the maintenance of cash flow and the settlement of purchase bills; and while these would be more than covered by the eventual sales of crops, flocks and herds, it was not always possible to predict with certainty when payments would be made, or how much payments would be.

This approach was reflected throughout the farming industry in the 1960s and 1970s. In 1984, following a series of expensive and high-profile bankruptcies and total losses, one of the London clearing banks changed its policy towards small and medium-sized rural businesses. Overdraft facilities would be prescribed. Flexibility would be allowed no longer. This would be underpinned by a refusal to pay or underwrite particular bills in the short-to-medium-term.

In the case of the farm in question, the bank manager was moved on. He was replaced by someone committed to implementing the new bank policy as summarised above.

Accordingly, the particular farming company was made bankrupt as the result of the bank's refusal to sanction a £9,000 payment for seeds and fertilisers. The feed and fertiliser supplier was invited to apply to the High Court for a bankruptcy order against the farm, and this was forthcoming.

The bank would have received its money in three months' time and there would have been no further problems; the situation would have gone on very much as before, though the returns available from the farming industry were declining.

This process was repeated with four other farms in the region. In two cases, the bank had 100 per cent charges on the bankruptcies; in the other cases, the charge was at least 50 per cent. The farms were sold on by the Official Receiver, together with other assets, in order to minimise the loss. However, these sales did not cover either the bank's total charge, nor the costs incurred as a result of not servicing the overdraft facilities.

Nevertheless, the manager who had pulled out of each of these ventures was rewarded. She was promoted from managing a small rural branch to a corporate position at the bank's headquarters in London, where she became part of the team driving overall strategy.

Box 8.6 *Insurance of finance: examples*

- *Aerospace*: There is an inherent attractiveness in investing in the civil and defence aviation industries because projects and ventures are underwritten by both the European Union and also the national governments of the Member States.
- *Tourism*: By contrast, the margins available in the package tour sector of the travel and tourism industry are so narrow that companies may go out of business as a result of minor fluctuations in currency prices. In 1998 two charter airlines and four travel agencies based in the UK all ceased trading as the result of the halving of the value of the Turkish lire against the UK pound. Their problems were exacerbated also by substantial devaluations in the value of the Spanish peseta, the Italian lire, and the Greek drachma. The tourist industry is underwritten by the Association of British Travel Agents (ABTA) but only to the extent of ensuring that tourists who are stranded as the result of bankruptcy can get home.

The contrasting outputs of these two examples demonstrate the attractiveness and security that arises as the result of the ability to fully underwrite or insure the finance necessary for the completion of the venture. In order for this to be fully effective however, a continuing professional (and therefore personal) relationship has to be established, maintained and delivered between those providing money for the venture, and those underwriting it. That way the underwriters understand the full extent of their liability and also the potential likelihood of their being asked to redeem the insurance policy.

Box 8.7 *The effective management of environmental lobbies*

Shell

Brent Spar, the oil rig owned by the Shell Company, came to the end of its useful life in the North Sea in 1990. It was proposed that the rig be towed out into the deepest part of the Atlantic and then sunk. The effluent present in the rig would be dispersed and there would be no visible or residual damage to either marine life or the human population.

The environmental lobbies responded as follows. They organised a boycott of the company's products; and especially created picket lines outside particular retail petrol outlets. This was only marginally successful in the UK; on the other hand, the company lost 44 per cent of sale in one weekend (and has never fully recovered since). This was supported by an information and advertising campaign drawing attention to the company's other activities (including dumping of toxic effluent in the Niger Delta).

In the matter of Brent Spar, the company was forced to re-think its strategy. The rig was towed to a quiet spot in Norway, while the company designed equipment with the purpose of breaking the rig up into components small enough to be disposed of on the land.

The UK Nuclear Industry

In 1998 members of an environmental lobby were able to observe the passage of a train carrying nuclear waste from the Dungeness nuclear power station in Kent, to Sellafield in Cumbria.

For the first 14 miles of the journey, the train was observed travelling on a badly maintained and overgrown railway line, on which it was subsequently found that 60 per cent of the railway sleepers were rotten. The line had not been upgraded for 17 years. British Nuclear Fuels, the owners and operators of the stretch of line, denied that there was any question of public safety. However, work started on refurbishing the line the week after the protestors gained an audience for their concerns.

Motorway Construction Schemes

Motorway construction schemes are always a concern to environmental lobbies because they are built through existing rural areas. They also bring with them construction blight during the period of their construction (which may take years) and residual blight, especially noise and exhaust pollution caused by their subsequent usage.

One such scheme constituted the construction of the M5 spur between Exeter and Honiton in Devon. There were mass protests from both environmental lobbies and residents' associations. Extensive and sympathetic media coverage was generated. The environmentalists invited journalists into the areas that they were occupying and demonstrated the lengths to which they were prepared to go to support something that was important to them.

This was contrasted by the refusal of the main contractors or the Department of Transport, the Environment and the Regions to present their point of view and to demonstrate the benefits of the scheme that were known, believed or perceived to accrue to everybody, including residents, once the motorway spur was completed.

A Note on Politicians

Dealing effectively with politicians in investment ventures requires a complete understanding of the position from which they are seeking to commission or enter the venture. In terms of influence, politicians are always the dominant partner. Invariably also, the primary return on investment sought by politicians is in terms of political drives and pressures, the need for triumphs, to *be seen to be* doing things, and because of pressures brought about by their representative role or echelons further up the hierarchy of their political party.

As important is the speed at which political drives and priorities change. Some of this is due to factors outside the politician's control. Factors to be especially aware of are timescale and quality changes, deadline shifts (especially delays and deferments for capital public works projects), rule changes (especially for investment in private finance initiative type ventures) and price and budget cuts.

The value of investments is also affected by changes in currency values, interest rates and the volume, range and attractiveness of investments such as government guilds and government bonds on offer. Governments also affect land, capital, property, commodity and goods prices through the use of public investment policies (see Chapter 2).

As a result of all of these points, politicians change their commitment, respect and loyalty to particular ventures overnight. Where the politician has made promises or commitments from a point of view of complete integrity, these may nevertheless have to be changed because of orders or direction from the political party, or because of changes in political priorities. Sudden bursts of inflation or serious interest rate increases mean that work promised is no longer viable.

Box 8.8   *Over-Mighty Individuals*

C5

The C5 was designed as a means of personal transport by the Sinclair
organisation. It was the brainchild of the company's founder and
major shareholder, Sir Clive Sinclair. Known to be a brilliant, creative
and inventive individual, he had earned a business reputation and
fortune by being one of the earliest players in the computer games
market.

The C5 was an electric three-wheeler buggy designed to ensure that
people could get themselves around urban areas and make short
journeys without having to use their cars or public transport. Substantial investment was attracted, the media interest was engaged, and
everyone looked confidently forward to the day when the C5 would be
the universally accepted way of travelling around towns.

The venture failed for the following reasons.

- The C5 was about the total size of a domestic sofa with a single
  wheel at the front and two at the back. It could only accommodate
  one person and there was no room for luggage. It sat very low near
  the ground; and the result was that those who drove them were at
  approximately wheel-hub height to the rest of the traffic (and also at
  approximately exhaust pipe height).
- It would travel at a maximum 10 miles per hour, with a cruising
  speed of approximately 7 miles per hour. The driver was not
  enclosed inside the machine, which meant that it could not be used
  except when the weather was good and when there was nothing else
  on the roads.

Because of the key influence of Sinclair, and the media presentation of
the project, none of the above became apparent until the prototypes
were tested.

Plastic Roads

In 1990 work was commissioned by the Department of Transport to
investigate the feasibility and viability of using plastic extrusion as the
means for producing highway infrastructure. Research was carried out
that demonstrated that this was indeed cheaper, more viable and much
quicker to complete than existing techniques using aggregate concrete

and tarmac. Moreover, the researchers reinforced their findings by stating that this would be a quick and cost-effective way of developing the transport infrastructure in countries such as China and India.

In 1998 the process was piloted in Marylebone Road, London. Within three months the process had to be scrapped for the following reasons.

- It was much noisier than the existing standard tarmacadam surface.
- It could not stand slow-moving traffic (and therefore would not be able to stand fast-moving traffic).
- It could not stand London volumes of traffic (and would therefore not be able to stand potential volumes of traffic in India and China generated by much greater population size and therefore much greater potential long-term car ownership).
- Within three months the surface itself was beginning to break up.
- The effects of extreme weather on the surface had not been tested.

The research was commissioned by a government agency, and because the researcher was one of the two most prestigious institutions in the UK, nobody sought to question whether or not these matters were capable of long-term sustained viability until the scheme was piloted.

A Note on Inward Investors

Of equal importance, though from a different perspective, is managing the introduction of inward investment.

Inward investment is the process by which governments attract overseas or out-of-region companies and organisations to establish their activities in a particular location, often to regenerate a measure of prosperity, or to create jobs in areas of high unemployment. This then acts as a multiplier or pump-primer for the generation of other activities.

The inward investor is over-mighty because of the sudden volume of financial and other resources that it brings and demands. As a result of this, it may have extensive knock-on effects on terms and conditions of employment, labour availability or labour relations for those already operating in the particular locality. Inward investors therefore exert in many situations an over-mightiness that is limited only by their own integrity and willingness to integrate into the rest of the business and wider position of the community (see box 8.9).

Box 8.9   *Hyundai in Scotland*

In 1986 Hyundai, the South Korean manufacturing, electronics and transport group, established a small management and research office in Dunfermline, Fife, Scotland. In 1994, following a boom in the world demand for microchips, it commenced building a £1.3 billion manufacturing plant at the location. This was to satisfy the boom in the computer market and to make sure that it maintained its share of the microchip output.

In 1997, following increasing high levels of demand for its products, the company announced the construction of a corporate infrastructure that would support four factories in the area. So long as market conditions remained good, the company stated that it would take its total investment to £2.6 billion and this would include the creation of a total of 3,200 jobs. This would make the particular venture one of the largest inward investment projects in the world.

The company also wished to use the facility for pioneering work on 64-megabyte memory chips and to investigate the feasibility of developing commercially viable 256-megabyte chips within two years. The company committed itself in October 1997 to the opening of a second factory, additional to its original £1.3 billion investment.

Other companies operating in the area immediately panicked. They foresaw fierce competition for labour, on the wage levels that Hyundai were prepared to pay (which were extremely good both for the locality and the sector), and were also concerned that there was insufficient expertise available in the location. The result would therefore be effectively an auction for expertise; and smaller companies were afraid that they would be unable to compete.

Accordingly, companies already in operation in the area took steps to ensure the loyalty of their staff through the creation of attractive bonus, profit sharing, profit-related and share-ownership schemes to try and ensure that when Hyundai did open their new venture, it would be more difficult for existing staff to go and join them.

Alongside this, extensive housing developments were commissioned. Two ventures of 700 luxury homes, together with 2,500 medium-quality houses were commissioned in rural greenbelt sites on the edge of Dunfermline. Also commissioned were sports facilities, a sports centre, a cricket ground, multiplex cinema and 62-acre rural leisure park.

This illustrates the extent of the capability of an organisation such as Hyundai to dominate the particular locations in which they seek to invest. In this particular case the problem was compounded by Hyundai first delaying, and then postponing indefinitely, any of this investment because of the currency crash in the Far East in 1998.

CONCLUSIONS

The purpose of this hapter has been to illustrate the effects that professional and personal relations have on the success or otherwise of investment ventures.

Where long-term, steady-state and enduring relationships are established, the need is only to recognise the importance of the relationships on which this is, at least in part, based, and to take steps to ensure that this is maintained and developed.

It is a key feature of the success of ventures when parties are coming together for the first time. The venture ultimately will only be successful if confidence, harmony and respect are maintained. Attention to each of the points indicated in this chapter is therefore essential. This must be a priority for all those directly involved; and it should be a priority for the other key players indicated. Especially, it is a part of the process that is neglected by shareholders and backer's representatives, and by over-mighty players; in many cases, it is apparent that they push through their own partial interest because they can, rather than because the overall demands of the venture require it.

9 Managing Investment Priorities

INTRODUCTION

Everything covered thus far has been concerned with drawing attention to each of the conditions necessary if successful ventures are to be considered. Each element – finance, strategy, the behavioural aspects, measurement and risk – has then to be considered in terms of the priorities and drives that are present in all ventures. These are:

- results;
- financial payments and repayments;
- non-financial repayments;
- operational relationships;
- the management of crises and contingencies;
- terminating investments and investment relationships.

The value mix and importance of each of these elements varies between ventures. However, they are all present in all ventures to a greater or lesser extent, and therefore require full consideration.

RESULTS

No investment venture or relationship is ever fully effective unless it is results-driven and results-oriented. This reinforces the need for everyone involved to know what they expect from the venture, and the expectation of the others involved; and for everyone concerned to be confident that these different expectations can be reconciled.

Problems arise when it becomes apparent or is perceived that:

- the results required or desired are not going to be achieved, either overall or in the desired timescale, or both;
- some of those involved will achieve their aims and objectives, but others will not;
- some of those involved will achieve their aims and objectives at the expense of others.

When this happens, any gaps in the integrity of relationships instantly become apparent. As a consequence, it is very easy for everything to be called into question. It can destroy a relationship, and damage (and sometimes indeed destroy) the venture. Dominant players exert their dominance and this invariably means looking after their own interests; this may or may not be at the expense of others involved. Minor or dependent players begin to bewail their lot, and seek media coverage for their own position if they cannot gain satisfaction from the venture itself (see box 9.1).

The demonstration of successful and effective results means that the parties to a particular venture are attractive to other initiatives in the future. It also means that there is a clear basis for establishing why, and how, things work so well.

FINANCIAL PAYMENTS AND REPAYMENTS

Closely related to results are the regularity, frequency and levels of repayments desired, incurred and achieved. The actuality of these reflects the quality of forecasting and planning. It also reflects the professional aspects of the relationship, because payment and repayment levels and intervals need to be established at the outset and then delivered as agreed. To fail to do so damages wider confidence in the venture. This may also lead to damaging and destroying relationships between those involved. It calls into question the genuineness of the reasons for being involved.

If this part of the process is not seen as a priority, then this leads to a proliferation of complaints and in-fighting. In large ventures, sub-groups and clusters of those involved become embroiled in personal and professional gossip concerning the integrity and tenacity of parties involved but excluded from the circle of conversation. This may lead to censure and attempts to renegotiate or downgrade the rewards available to one or more of those involved. In the financial services industry, this is a major source of complaints to regulatory authorities and ombudsmen.

Perceptions are also important. If one party is presented with a rate of return, and levels and frequency of payment, which initially appear attractive, this will hold good only as long as the repayment frequencies and levels last. If levels drop, they may insist on the original agreement being fulfilled, even though this may jeopardise the performance of the rest of the venture and levels of payment agreed with other parties.

If return on investment vastly exceeds expectations, however, they may feel that they were never given the full picture at the outset. They thus perceive that their expectations were set at levels too low. They will then question why this should have been. It may, for example, be that the levels were truly realistic, but that circumstances changed, or that the venture proved supremely attractive once it was committed to purpose. Or they may come to believe that by accepting guaranteed low rates of return, any additional surpluses would then be commanded by other more powerful interests in the venture. Or they may wonder whether the others involved, especially the dominant partners, really knew what they were doing.

Box 9.1 *Problems with investment in pension schemes*

Individuals invest in pension schemes to provide an adequate standard of living for their old age and post-employment period of life. Companies invest in pension schemes to take advantage of tax benefits, and because business is perceived to be both continuous and expanding (everyone needs provision for their later years); they also invest in pension schemes to provide an adequate standard of living for those in their later years. There is therefore a clear divergence of objectives; and a clearly dominant-dependent relationship.

This has led to companies borrowing from their own pension schemes in times of cash flow or venture capital difficulties (the most notorious example of which was Robert Maxwell, who stole from his employees' pension schemes). Companies changed the rules governing pension schemes according to what is deemed to be a *satisfactory* standard of pension provided for the individual pensioners; this invariably means that the payments are reduced. The tax advantages only accrue at the point of payment into the pension schemes; there are no tax advantages in payments out or receipts.

The problem has been exacerbated in recent years by the mis-selling and mis-projection of returns available. In the worst cases, this has been carried out as a result of drives for maximised, committed, long-term income on the part of those who may have anything up to 40 years' working life remaining. As there is now no prospect of steady, regularised increases in payment for employment, the difficulties may not become apparent for 20 years, when people are forced to take reductions in employment payment, under conditions created and enforced through statutes by government, and reinforced by the companies whose responsibility it is to invest the funds.

Companies have also sought to exclude certain categories of pensioners from any corporate responsibility, in spite of the fact that they paid into schemes over the period of their employment. The most notorious example of this is the National Bus Company pension scheme. When the company was privatised, the new owners sought to absolve themselves of responsibilities for making pension payments to anybody who subsequently joined the company; and to reduce payments to those who had already ceased working. First brought to the attention of government in 1989, the matter was not fully resolved until August 1999, when the company was required by court judgment to accept the full range of responsibilities inherent in the scheme, and to appoint a pensioners' representative, as required by the rules of the scheme. Moreover, this was only brought to the attention of the public at large at all because one pensioner made it his business to engage the media interest, and to seek support for a legal challenge to a position which was eventually only changed after a ten-year campaign. Ultimately, the only beneficiaries of this dispute were accountants, lawyers and consultants, each engaged by the different parties at great expense to fight and argue the particular cases from a partial – rather than enlightened – point of view.

The effect of variations in payments and repayments is often a lesser concern to the financial interests because they can effectively cut off their contribution to the resources at any time (even if this subsequently leads to litigation). This is especially true where they are also the dominant interest. However, in the longer term, to fail to be concerned with levels of regularity and frequency of payments is extremely damaging because people will only seek support from institutions taking this attitude if they really have to do so.

Conversely, questions of payments and repayments are very high on the list of priorities to be addressed by the non-financial interests involved because they are only going to reap the full benefits if expectations are set at a practical level (see box 9.2).

Establishing the levels of financial payments and returns is a key output of effective forecasting. When addressing this priority, the results of forecasting techniques must be presented in such ways as to indicate:

- the levels of return available
- the regularity and frequency with which payments are to be made
- matters within the sector that may cause the levels, regularity and frequency to change
- the effects of substitution alternatives on venture performance
- the effects of problems on the supply side or distribution side on venture performance.

This can then be related to net present value and other pre-assessment techniques, to ensure that the financial returns levels and frequency of payments are basically feasible in the context of the particular venture, and the environment in which it is being carried out.

Box 9.2   *Financial payments*

Share Dividends

Share dividends are normally paid out of profits on activities and ventures over the period of a year to shareholders as a reward for placing their funds in the particular venture or company, and as a key part of their return on investment (the price of a share is the other part of this return). In simple terms, as the result of having had a good year, dividends are high; and when the year's results are poor, dividends are low or non-existent.

In recent years, however, it has come to be a part of accepted shareholder management that minimum dividend levels will be guaranteed, even through bad years. This means that a proportion of profits retained and accrued from previous years, or else share capital, is being used to pay dividends to shareholders.

The advantage of this is that companies have at least been forced to take a long-term view of shareholder interest. In many cases, however, this is more than offset by the fact that to fail to pay these dividends out of pre-retained profits and share capital would simply cause a loss of confidence in the company or venture as shareholders sought to divest their interest in favour of something more profitable elsewhere.

This is reinforced by the belief and perception that, also in recent years, share-ownership buying and selling has become an industry all of its own. The result is that shareholder expectations have been greatly increased; venture loyalty has decreased; and this has compounded the problems already inherent in seeking to establish assured long-term funds.

NON-FINANCIAL REPAYMENTS

The question of non-financial repayments is also complex. Non-financial repayments are directly affected by the financial performance of the venture. The areas of overlap between the two are confidence and expectations (see Figure 9.1).

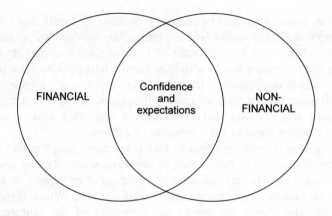

Figure 9.1 *The relationship between financial and non-financial repayments*

Distributive Repayments

Distributive repayments occur where:

- one party receives their repayment at the expense of others
- one party is able to command greater levels of repayment at the expense of others
- one party imposes a condition of priority repayments at the expense of others
- one party succeeds by dominating the venture at the expense of others.

In non-financial terms, consideration of the distributive aspect is of critical importance because it highlights the basic integrity of the relationship. Especially where one party has dominated the whole of the venture, they are likely to take the lion's share of the credit, prestige, kudos and profile, as well as the financial returns. They may also claim credit for the success of the total venture, even though others had made small but critical interventions.

Dominant partners may also feel themselves strong and powerful enough to discredit the other parties to the venture should anything go wrong. They seek to belittle the contribution of others, in extreme cases calling into question their commitment and expertise.

Security

This refers to the security of the venture itself; and also to the security of involvement. Again, in many cases, this is called into question by matters of perception, rather than fact or certainty. Security, integrity and confidence in ventures is always raised when a particular contingency or emergency occurs which has not been thought of in advance. Or it may be that one member of the venture has to withdraw for the best possible reasons, or for matters outside their control. In any of these cases, those involved (or still involved) make the connection between the present set of circumstances and the returns and rewards that are available; and they almost invariably question whether these are still possible to achieve.

Security is more of a problem in fact when more tangible factors come into force. For example, full success of the venture may depend upon being able to secure a particular commodity, component or supply; or to secure sources of finance from particular named sources. When these fail to materialise, then there are questions of security of the venture, and of involvement, that have to be addressed. If finance is required from particular or named sources, then the propensity of these institutions to support ventures from inception to completion has to be assessed, and relationships with them developed on this basis. If other sources are to be used, then the policy of those institutions towards supporting ventures from inception to completion, and their propensity and readiness to move funds in and out of ventures in pursuit of their own shorter-term objectives, must be assessed.

The following other matters need to be addressed.

Reputation

This involves the nature of the reputation accrued and the effects of this (whether positive or negative) on future ventures. Effects on reputation as the result of involvement in ventures are:

- enhancement – if the venture is known, believed, perceived or capable of being presented as having achieved all of the aims and objectives of those involved;
- dilution – if the venture does not live up to expectations;
- destruction – if the venture fails, or if there is a scandal around the venture which destroys public confidence.

Reputation may also become sullied if there are ethical or environmental issues which subsequently become apparent, or which are brought to the public's attention through whistle-blowing or the activities of pressure groups and lobbies.

Reputation may also be lost or damaged as the result of non-venture association (see box 9.3).

Box 9.3 *London Regional Transport and the London Underground system*

Over the period since 1980, the London Underground mass transit passenger railway system has 'got much worse'. That is the summary belief and perception of all those who use it, and of many who work on it.

Over the period, the system has been the subject of repairs, upgrading of facilities, and replacement of trains. The drive for this has been:

- partly political, as part of the policy of removing private cars from the streets of London during working hours as far as possible;
- partly consumer led, because they expect services to improve, especially when compared with fare levels which have steadily increased;
- partly technological, because new improved cost-effective railway technology is now available – though at a price.

Towards the end of the period, London Regional Transport's policy towards refurbishment and upgrade has been to shut down particular sections of the network and to refurbish these fully before reopening them. This has led to short-term extensive passenger inconvenience, and loss of respect and reputation for the network as a whole.

Problems with this approach have been compounded by the refusal of government to increase levels of public investment in making the network effective. The company has therefore had to draw on pre-retained surpluses, surpluses accrued through fare increases, and borrowings on the commercial markets. This has hampered the development of the system and the policy objectives stated.

The company has also undertaken extensive pioneering work to enlarge the system. This commenced at the beginning of the period with the creation of the Docklands Light Railway; and, in more recent times, the extension to the Jubilee Line which is now to terminate at Greenwich near the site of the Millenium Dome.

The company has therefore clearly carried out extensive investment in its own future. The net result is, however, that the reputation of the service for being reliable and punctual has largely been lost; and this is a direct result of the investment approach imposed on the company, and the short-term outputs that have accrued as the result.

Reputation is also dependent upon presenting the case for investment effectively, as well as making sure that it is sound in conception. It underlines the importance of both media and the public at large as stakeholders and vested interests in their own right, because initial or continuing adverse publicity is certain to influence general public reception and confidence. As stated above, managing these groups effectively is a key part of ensuring that the venture is indeed successful in the terms in which it was devised. A major non-financial return is the reception accorded to ventures at all stages – design, inception and commitment; and the consequent positive or negative association of those involved (see box 9.4).

Box 9.4　*The Child Support Agency*

The Child Support Agency was conceived in 1990 by the UK Conservative Government. It had the aim of ensuring that children were fully and adequately supported by both their parents, whether or not they continued to live together. As most absent parents were fathers, this quickly became a perceived drive to make absent fathers acknowledge, and pay for, their responsibilities towards their children.

The proposal was met with almost universal approval. The agency was created in 1992 commencing operations on 1 April that year. The order of public investments was £2 billion, and it was ordered in the first full year of operations to recoup £500 million from absent fathers and thus reduce the burden on the social security benefit system by that amount.

It quickly ran into difficulties. The Chief Executive had no experience of dealing with public service clients. The computer system was incapable of accessing existing social security, child support or social services records. A policy decision was taken that public servants experienced in dealing with these client groups would not be employed; those responsible for dealing with the public would effectively be telephone experts. Public contact would be conducted entirely through the telephone, using computer records to support the points being made in dealings with the particular clients. In order to get over the problem of lack of information, a 32-page form was devised. Initially, in 96 per cent of cases this form was inaccurately filled in.

In November 1994, following repeated failures to meet income targets, a policy decision was taken to chase 'easy and profitable targets'. Recalcitrant fathers were therefore ignored. Efforts were concentrated on medium- to high-income fathers whose whereabouts were known, and who, in many cases, had already acknowledged their responsibilities and were paying what they could.

The result of this was to engage articulate professional men in a universal national lobby. Newspaper and television journalists fell into the category now being chased, and therefore were only too keen to project their stories. It quickly became apparent that the Child Support Agency was failing to act with the integrity with which it had been first endowed; and that it had simply become a fundraising organisation. Where these funds came from did not matter so long as they were raised. The Agency consequently fell into disrepute and is certain either to be abolished or substantially reconstituted prior to the general election date of 2002.

In political terms, there was an instant payback when the idea was first proposed, and the Agency first created. The reputation of both government and officials was substantially enhanced. By 1994, however, this reputation had been completely destroyed, as had the career of Alan Burn, the junior minister responsible for steering the project to completion. He resigned in early 1995, stating that he would be unable to command a majority if it came to a vote of confidence in either himself or the Agency. The Social Security Secretary under whose overall authority the Agency was established, distanced himself from it as quickly as he possibly could.

One result of the adverse media coverage was to highlight the incidents with which the Agency made incorrect calculations. The admitted and agreed figure is that 96 per cent of calculations are inaccurate. Because of this:

- people now only go the Agency when they are forced to;
- people go to the Agency on the basis that they will be badly treated;
- people go to the Agency in the belief that calculations will be wrong.

All this has happened as the result of loss of reputation in a venture that had universal public support at its outset.

OPERATIONAL RELATIONSHIPS

In investment appraisal, as in all aspects of business and management, working relationships are only fully effective if they are based on:

- mutuality of interest
- trust, integrity, honesty and openness
- availability of high-quality information

- general access and visibility
- coincidence of purpose and unity of overall direction.

Building, developing and managing these relations is founded on a series of regular, structured, face-to-face meetings between named representatives of all the parties involved in the venture. These meetings need authority to act in the best interests of the venture and to take whatever decisions are necessary.

It is essential that there is extensive consultation with all those involved who are going to be responsible for directing, guiding and completing different parts of the venture is required special reference to problems of differences in management style and organisational and operational culture.

It is also necessary to pay full attention to operational details on which the success of the venture may depend (see box 9.5).

An attitude to problems that acknowledges that they are going to arise and engages a positive commitment to getting them resolved without recourse to claim and counterclaim, re-negotiation of venture arrangements, or litigation.

The key to this lies in the overall confidence held in the venture. If these conditions are not present, working relationships are not going to be generated that build on and reinforce this confidence. The success of any venture always lies in the clarity of purpose and direction of all those involved in pursuit of effective and profitable ventures; and this is only engaged if time and resources are taken at the inception to ensure as full an understanding as possible.

Reporting relationships between those directly managing the investment, and their own organisations, consequently need to be simple and direct, and quick to operate when required. No investment ever benefits from delays caused by the operation of decision-making processes and administrative systems, and these, in turn, lead to frustration and, in some cases, to loss of confidence in the venture. Where there is no full understanding, any cracks in the unity of purpose of those involved become apparent whenever problems and issues arise. This applies to all parts of the process and at all stages of the venture.

Direct contact between key representatives also maintains all of the other aspects indicated. The greater the personal contact, the greater the professional confidence generated; conversely, where this is neither present nor perceived to be important, the effectiveness of the venture is reduced. And the lack of full confidence is always transmitted to operational staff during consultation or briefing meetings.

This then needs to be underpinned by other forms of communication and contact. It is not always possible to make face-to-face contact at other stages; therefore telephone, teleconferencing, fax and e-mail systems are required. These, however, must be used to support the relationship and should never become its basis. Above all, when problems and issues do become apparent, somebody acting with the full authority and backing of those directing the venture must always be available to visit the problem and address the concerns raised.

Box 9.5　*The Folkestone–Dover railway line*

This stretch of railway line carries passengers from the port of Dover to London for onward transition to other parts of the UK. It is also part of an extremely busy commuter line; starting at Sandwich in Kent, and working its way around the Kent coast through Dover and Folkestone, it carries upwards of 50,000 passengers per day along the length of its line, both into and out of London.

It is usual for the line to be fully open for the period Monday–Friday of each week; maintenance and upgrade is then scheduled for the weekends. Where necessary, replacement bus services are provided while work is being carried out on the railway line.

In April 1998, Railtrack plc, the owners of the stretch of railway line between Folkestone and Dover, engaged a new main contractor to carry out maintenance and refurbishment work. This company had undercut the existing contractor by 10 per cent; and was accordingly engaged.

At the end of the first weekend's work, the new contractor met with Railtrack representatives to inspect and agree that the work had been completed to the required standard.

Initial inspection found that the live electricity rail had not been replaced; inspection of the contract and service standards agreed found that the requirement to replace the third rail had been omitted.

There was consequently serious disruption to services for the Monday, Tuesday and Wednesday of the following week while the matter was put right. Compensation and alternative forms of transport provided to regular customers far outweighed the 10 per cent saving made.

The main reason why this failed so spectacularly was that the working relationship was founded only on the 10 per cent discount. No provision for anything else had been agreed; the subcontractor was keen to get started (and therefore to get paid), and Railtrack were keen to demonstrate a 10 per cent saving. This was the entire driving force behind the relationship; and the overwhelming reason why Railtrack had seen fit to cancel the contract of expert railway engineers, many of whom had worked for British Rail, the previously nationalised company, for many years.

Investment Appraisal

THE MANAGEMENT OF CRISES AND CONTINGENCIES

If the working relationship is established successfully, crises and contingencies become much easier to forecast and plan for. They are easier to identify, and can be recognised early, and then steps taken to nip them in the bud. The consequence is that a genuine crisis is both rare and the outcome of genuinely unforeseen circumstances (see box 9.6).

Box 9.6 *Hong Kong International Airport*

The Hong Kong International Airport was built by a consortium of Far Eastern and Western construction companies. Finance was provided by the governments of the European Union and the banking and finance sector in Hong Kong. The airport was completed in June 1997, and handed over to the Chinese authorities, who were to take charge of it at the same time as Hong Kong was returned to their jurisdiction.

Problems became apparent immediately the airport was opened. The glass used as cladding for the main terminal building was not adequate to reflect the heat from the sun, and the air conditioning was not strong enough to counteract this; at one point in September 1997, the temperature inside the building rose to 48° centigrade. The glass cladding had therefore to be replaced.

Airports draw their revenues from throughputs of passengers, handling charges, and commercial and duty-free sales.

In August 1999 a Cathay Pacific Boeing 747 attempted to land at the airport during a typhoon. As it came in to land, the airliner was blown off course and finished up on its side with a broken wing. That only 22 people out of the 430 on board lost their lives was described as 'a miracle' by the CNN reporter on the spot.

Both of these events could have been foreseen. In particular there was no reason for the problem with the glass cladding to occur. However, the political and financial drives for completion on the scheduled deadline overrode any considerations of project quality or durability. The result, however, is that this refurbishment will not be completed until the Year 2002; and that this will result in long and complex litigation between financiers and the different construction companies to determine who is ultimately responsible for this failure, and to seek compensation and damages.

This is a key part of the effective assessment and management of risk (see Chapter 7). However, the relationship must be of sufficient openness and integrity to ensure that when potential problems do become apparent, they are recognised and dealt with from a point of view of mutuality of interest rather than blame. It is also much easier to assess the levels of contingency funding necessary if the working relationship is right because the extent and potential threat of crises will be assessed on the basis of reality rather than on perceived acceptability.

Assessment of the possibility of crises, and the levels of contingency funding required as a result, clearly depend on:

- the sector or sectors in which investment is being made
- the attitudes of the parties involved to the provision of contingency funding
- openness of pre-planning, research and forecasting approaches
- sectoral factors
- any particular issues relating to the location in which the venture is to be carried out, especially political, social or economic instability.

The nature and mix of each of these points will clearly vary between ventures; nevertheless, each needs consideration in the particular context in which investment is being made so that a recent and informed view of the requirement for contingency funding can be established.

TERMINATING INVESTMENTS AND INVESTMENT RELATIONSHIPS

Investments are terminated for the following reasons.

- completion of the venture (e.g. capital projects, computer and information technology projects);
- completion of the phase of the venture in which one or more parties are involved;
- lack of expertise or knowledge in what is now feasible;
- lack of resources to pursue the partnership further;
- lack of professional or managerial desire to pursue the partnership further.

Taken from a positive point of view, each aspect is completely legitimate and should be recognised as such. It is essential that termination arrangements are built into contracting formats. This includes arrangements for final payments and returns, and also any residual entitlement such as the ability to use involvement in the venture for future marketing or prospectus purposes or to use technology that has been brought into the venture for other purposes.

Otherwise, investment ventures and relationships are terminated because:

- it becomes apparent that there are secondary, subsidiary or hidden agenda which other parties to the venture cannot support;
- one or more of the parties involved comes to dominate the venture and use it for its own ends in ways that the others find unacceptable;
- one or more parties find that they can no longer afford to be involved in the venture;
- evidence of dishonesty is brought to light; disputes and litigation between some of the parties has the effect of destroying the rest of the relationship;
- there are extensive professional and personality clashes (see box 9.7).

Box 9.7   *Glaxo-Wellcome and SmithKline Beecham*

In 1996 a merger was proposed between Glaxo-Wellcome and SmithKline Beecham, the two largest drug and pharmaceutical companies in the world. The effects of this merger would have been to create the third largest company in the world. The value of the venture was calculated at £100 billion.

The venture failed because the 12 people responsible for guiding the venture through to completion could not agree on who was to do which job in the new merged organisation. It was finally agreed to proceed with the venture in February 2000.

Aims and Objectives in Termination

So long as the relationship has been established with integrity, aims and objectives in termination simply consist of reviewing the venture, dividing the returns and assessing the results so that everyone involved is satisfied; and, where necessary, assessing any shortfalls so that at least the reasons for these are apparent. A further aim is to keep open general channels of communication in case further opportunities present themselves in the future.

Problems arise where these conditions do not exist. A major concern of investors is the ability to at least get back their money (or expertise or other resources) if the venture goes wrong. All concerned have their reputations to protect and will try and withdraw from ventures if it becomes apparent that these will be damaged by remaining. Lobbies and pressure groups try, in some circumstances, to work on the most vulnerable parties with the purpose of destroying their confidence and involvement in particular ventures (see box 9.8).

Box 9.8 *Animal rights and the pharmaceutical industry*

A key part of medical research and investigation over the period since 1930 has involved vivisection (cutting up live animals under anaesthetic), and the testing of drugs and cosmetics on animals to assess them for effectiveness and side-effects. People have always been concerned with the ethics of this since it was first commenced; however, at the outset there was a social perception that the value to humanity outweighed the suffering caused to animals.

Animal rights lobbies first became influential in the late 1960s in the UK and subsequently grew in influence over the following 20 years. However, although they had raised public awareness, effects of lobbying and picketing the major drug and pharmaceutical companies, and of trying to persuade consumers not to buy the products, proved ineffective.

Accordingly, the animal rights lobby turned its attention to the farms that bred animals for onward sale to the pharmaceutical companies for the specific intention of experimentation. This is much more effective. It forced the drug and pharmaceutical companies, especially those engaged in research, to seek alternative means of pre-testing their products before they became available for human testing and, subsequently, for commercialisation. It has also begun to concentrate efforts on corporate investors in these companies.

Above all, nobody wants to find themselves in the position where they can effectively neither stay in the venture nor leave it. This has happened in diverse examples as follows.

- *Eurotunnel*: where the size of the capital debt is too large for the backers involved to withdraw.
- *Tour operators in Turkey*: who find that because of the national currency collapse, they cannot be adequately paid in local currency because it is not

worth enough; nor can they insist on being paid in hard currency because the local currency will not buy enough of it.

- *Personal pension schemes*: which, in many cases, are not delivering the benefits promised, but will not deliver anything at all if the investor ceases to make payments.

So it is essential to ensure that the ending of the relationship is seen as a priority. It can then be managed as a key part of the process. The problems and issues indicated above also become more apparent at an earlier stage if the ending of the relationship is acknowledged and given the attention necessary.

Confidence and Termination

It is also true that in the long term it is in nobody's interest to develop or gain a reputation as a bad party in ventures and investments. Clearing banks and some finance houses suffered from this in the UK during the 1970s and 1980s to such an extent that venture capitalists were able to grow their own sector in spite of the fact that they had neither local reputation nor track record.

Conversely, the UK civil engineering, construction and information technology sectors paid no attention to their reputation for late delivery, cost overruns and quality problems. Consequently, prospective clients and venturers looked elsewhere in the world for contractors and partners. Moreover, this took place during a period of time when the civil engineering and construction sectors were in decline; and when the information technology sector was becoming extremely competitive as both hardware and software prices fell sharply.

More generally, public confidence has been affected by problems associated with:

- real and perceived declines in public services, especially health, education and social services;
- increases in charges for water, gas, electricity and transport, together with perceptions and realities of declining services;
- declining public and private transport infrastructure;
- declining and unsatisfactory returns on personal investments, deposits and pensions. While it remains true that, at present, demand for each of these products and services is inelastic, this may change in the future and organisations at greatest long-term risk will be those that gave insufficient priority to these aspects of the investment process.

CONCLUSIONS

Identifying and addressing each of these areas as a priority ensures that concentration on the output requirement is maintained. It also reinforces the point that investment is a continuous process. People and organisations continually lay out money, expertise, time, energy and other resources in the expectation and anticipation of returns. The effective management of investment priorities is an excellent form of checking progress and the effectiveness with which these resources are being used. Understanding what the priorities are, and whether they are capable of achievement in the particular context, can only be arrived at through adopting a form of judgement and evaluation based on consideration of: returns; working relationships; contingencies; and acknowledgement that, when the venture comes to an end, the ending itself has also to be managed.

10   Implementing Investments

INTRODUCTION

The purpose of this chapter is to look in more detail at some of the major opportunities available to investors and venturers. The illustrations and examples so far considered indicate the range that is available to both individuals and organisations. It has also been stated throughout that investment is a continuous process.

So by bringing all of this together under specific headings, it is possible to see each of the elements necessary for successful ventures in action, and how they interact with each other. The areas considered are:

- personal investment and finances
- acquisitions, mergers and takeovers
- capital projects
- privatisation of public services and utilities
- other factors and issues.

PERSONAL INVESTMENTS AND FINANCES

Over the past 50 years in the UK there has been a fundamental cultural and social shift in attitudes to personal investment. Previously, the only long-term financial commitments were accommodation (either bought or rented), together with the real or perceived habit of making payments into building society deposit accounts with the purpose of building up small personal savings.

All that has changed. Bought accommodation is now normally supported by extensive mortgage arrangements and is viewed as an investment on which positive returns are expected. People are also now required to make enduring provision for insurances, old-age accommodation and pensions, savings and transport; and some also choose to invest as individuals in health care, education, childcare, shares and equity plans. So a substantial part of disposable income is tied up in regular and enduring financial commitments; and a large and sophisticated industry is now available to support this.

The key issue here is the working relationship between investors and providers. This is normally not well defined. Personal investors are not normally provided with clear, tangible or quantifiable rates of return on any of the matters indicated so far (see box 10.1).

This is compounded by:

- the presentation of investments by those making the offers
- the real or perceived dominance of providers of financial services in the relationship
- discouragement of the individual to become actively involved in the relationship
- lack of clarity of purpose of those who regulate the activities in the personal investment sector (see box 10.2).

If the principles indicated in previous chapters in the book are adopted, it becomes clear why the relationship is not normally effective. This may be summarised as follows.

- There is no clarity of definition of 'investor' and 'venturer'. Individuals as venturers are asked to accept many of the elements of risk that are accepted by the investor, or else spread, in commercial situations.
- Minimum rates of return are not offered by the financial services industry. The industry argues that when finance is required for life (e.g. health care, pensions – pension plans may endure for 90 years), it is impossible to guarantee any rate of return. Superficially it is a valid argument. However, the process, and support for this argument are not well supported by the financial services industry. Moreover, in commercial ventures, any risk of this nature would be acknowledged and the elements spread among all parties. Investing in personal finance requires that the entire risk is accepted by the venturer.
- No genuine working investor relationship exists. Institutions providing personal financial services are normally required to make at least an annual contact with their clients, and to provide statements of account. In commercial ventures, this would be unacceptable. In practice, in the personal services sector, this is the most that happens.
- Because the individual is making a personal rather than professional commitment, there exists no genuine scope for withdrawal or cancellation. Those who do so are blacklisted and may not be able to gain finance in the future. Those who withdraw from pension arrangements are penalised through a system of prescribed rather than agreed charges, and these may have been varied, or may subsequently be varied, without notification or consultation.
- Value for money and acceptable levels of return on investment are never defined (and not normally sought either).
- In addition, individual blacklisting and prohibition charges for these services are unilaterally established by the industry. This may be conducted on the basis of the individual's occupation, past history or association; or their place of work, location, postcode or address (see box 10.3).

Box 10.1   *Personal investments and finances: sample returns on invest-*
                ment itemised

- *Property prices*: The problem with regarding property as an investment is that it is impossible to project rates of return over even a
  short period of time; and this is compounded because most property
  investments are supported by mortgages repayable over periods of
  between 15 and 25 years. People are therefore asked to make a
  regular commitment to something on which there is no guaranteed
  rate of return at all; the normal fall-back is to regard projections of
  potential value as measures of actual worth. The problem would be
  removed at a stroke if property were to be seen as a high-value
  considered purchase, rather than an investment, as it is in many
  other parts of the world.
- *Pensions*: Pensions are sold on the basis of prescribed compulsory
  projections which financial services institutions are required by law
  to provide. Again, however, the boundaries in which returns are
  actually achievable are so wide as to be entirely unpredictable; and
  this is compounded by the fact that many pension plans are undertaken over periods of up to 50 years. As stated elsewhere, investors
  are being asked to make a regular and increasing commitment for
  outcomes that may or may not materialise.
- *Education*: Those paying into private education plans do so on the
  basis that any school and college fees required will be met by the
  plan. In practice this nearly always results in a subsidy only; the
  levels of premium required to guarantee the ability to meet the actual
  level of payment is always out-performed by making – and actively
  managing – ventures into unit trusts and personal equity plans, and
  using the returns on these to pay the education charges.
- *Privatisation shares*: Also as stated elsewhere, it has become impossible for personal investors to maximise long-term gains on these
  investments because of the legal obligation to sell to the new owners
  of the privatised companies under the provisions of the Companies
  Act 1988, stating that once an acquiring organisation has bought
  more than 90 per cent of shares, it is entitled to purchase the
  remainder at the current market rate.
- *Health care*: Those investing in private health care insurance have at
  least a range of benefits clearly set out to which they are entitled in
  return for making regular premium payments. They can then choose
  to buy the offering on the basis that they know what is on offer
  should they ever need it.

- *Interest rates on deposit accounts*: These are low enough to be guaranteed. However, they are still subject to variations by governments and national banking institutions.

When viewed in this way, it is apparent that the personal finance industry is asking individuals to make commitments that would simply not be tenable in corporate investment ventures. This is certain to become an increased matter of enduring concern to all involved. It is therefore extremely difficult to praise personal investments for: strategy, aims and objectives; risk; management; or relationship aspects. Standard investment appraisal techniques are of little value when trying to assess these particular ventures. This either means that new models have to be devised to satisfy the demands inherent in this sector; or else it means that 'personal investments' are a matter of considered purchase only, from which some satisfaction may be derived upon completion of the purchase (much more akin to the satisfaction derived from the consumption of groceries, rather than the outputs required and desired by corporate investment ventures).

Considered in this way, there is no prospect of genuine long-term mutuality of interest, satisfaction or achievement.

ACQUISITIONS, MERGERS AND TAKEOVERS

There are a number of legitimate reasons why these are considered as follows.

- to gain an interest in, or control of, a key source of, or outlet for, scarce raw materials, components, expertise or distribution;
- to gain control over supplies, components, distribution, outlets and access;
- to gain market share and market dominance; to maximise/optimise market opportunities;
- to gain new markets for existing products, services and expertise, or to bring new products, services and expertise to existing markets;
- to buy up a customer product or expertise base; to gain greater influence on quality, price and costs;
- to speed up the process of market penetration; to gain a foothold and then reputation in hitherto unfamiliar fields.

As long as the proposal can be legitimately considered from one or more of these points of view, then each of the main criteria can be satisfied. Strategy, policy, aims and objectives can be directly related to each of these points. The behavioural, cultural and relationship aspects can be assessed for costs and benefits. The extent of risk can be defined, as can measures by which the venture will be judged for success or failure.

Box 10.2   *The Personal Investment Authority*

The Personal Investment Authority (PIA) is a statutory body that has the role and function of regulating the investment activities and products available through the financial services industry. It is limited by:

- the requirement only to provide illustrations of growth rates, rather then clear indications of growth rates;
- a disclaimer to the effect that the value of investments can go down as well as up;
- lack of responsibility by those arranging the investment for the subsequent performance of the investment.

Mortgage investments are not regulated by the PIA. A charge on the mortgaged property is normally required in the event of inability to continue repayments, or to meet the full value of the mortgage. Other products, including life assurance, personal equity plans and investments, health care and school fees investment products may or may not be regulated by the PIA.

Individual financial services organisations are not required to give advice on the products that they offer for sale. They simply have their own portfolio which is effectively offered on a continuing retail basis to those wishing to avail themselves of the real or perceived opportunity.

No guaranteed minimum returns are available on any investment. While it may be argued that because of the nature of the finance industry at large this is not feasible, it remains true that for equivalent corporate investments (e.g. corporate mortgages, corporate pension schemes, corporate investment portfolios) it is possible to arrange guaranteed minimum rates of return.

Box 10.3 *The unilateral fixing of charges*

On three blacklisting or charging criteria – occupation, past history and address – the financial services industry was unable to provide data in 1999 to support the unilateral levels and variations in charges that it could command.

- *On occupation*: No significant data existed that demonstrated whether people working in a profession, occupation, semi-skilled or unskilled activities were more or less likely to maintain the terms of the investment or to withdraw from it. The industry pays little account, however, to those on incomes of less than £15,000 per annum, or those seeking to make investments of less than £5,000. Persons in this position are normally recommended to open bank or building society deposit accounts.
- *Past history*: The industry acknowledged that someone's history of breaking commitments in the past was no indication that they would do so in the future; nor that someone who had a good record of maintaining and servicing commitments in the past would continue to do so in the future. It is also acknowledged by the industry that there are no occupations in which it is possible to guarantee (*a*) income; (*b*) increases in income; (*c*) guaranteed security of payments into personal investment schemes.
- *Address*: The extreme form of 'managing by address' is exclusion or redlining, which is the process whereby financial institutions decide to exclude particular sectors of the population from access to their products. It is again acknowledged by the industry that this is a very crude form of market and investment management; and that again, living in a favoured area is no guarantee of successful business, nor is living in a redlined or excluded area any guarantee of unsuccessful business.

Source: Abbey National plc (1999); Standard Life (1999).

Problems with acquisitions, mergers and takeovers arise when one or more of the following applies:

- The proposal is acceptable to one dominant vested interest but not others. Invariably, this is driven by stock market and short-term shareholders' interests. The price of shares in the takeover target rises steeply. In many cases, so does the price of shares in the company carrying out the takeover. A point is reached at which existing shareholders are persuaded to sell their shares, achieving an instant return. The process is fuelled by stockbrokers and other shareholder representatives who gain commissions; and by rises in share prices in the acquiring company, because this is deemed or perceived to reflect the strategic acumen of its directors.

- The proposal is driven by certainties, hopes and expectations of 'synergies' or 'economies of scale', even though these are neither defined nor modelled. This approach becomes a substitute for investment appraisal; and is the overriding single reason why most such ventures either fail or fall short of full success (see box 10.4).
- Outline proposals are latched on to by one vested interest and then hyped up to the point at which they gain a life of their own. However effective any subsequent analysis and groundwork, professional knowledge and expertise becomes dominated by vested interest influence; and this is at its worst when the media or politicians are the vested interest in question.
- Outline proposals look superficially attractive and interest – especially partial and vested – is engaged. Subsequent analysis finds that the proposal is not sustainable, and yet there are behavioural or political reasons why the matter must now go ahead.
- The proposal is only sustainable up to the point at which the acquisition, merger or takeover is achieved. It then becomes immediately apparent that company cultures, technology, markets, ways of working, product performance are incompatible; and whatever short-term gains are made are more than offset by the problems that become immediately apparent.

Effective appraisal would bring all of these points to light if it were allowed to do so. Apart from drives based on 'certainties', the major cause of failure in these ventures is the over influence and over-drive of short-term powerful financial and political vested interests.

CAPITAL PROJECTS

To be fully effective, investment in capital projects requires a long-term commitment to purpose. Whether in building, construction, civil engineering, information systems or the internet, full and enduring project effectiveness is only achieved through a long-term strategic, rather than expectational, approach (see box 10.5).

Box 10.4 *CGU*

In 1990, at the height of a property boom, the then Commercial Union insurance company (now CGU) acquired a nation-wide chain of estate agencies. The justification for this was that it would provide additional outlets through which its insurance and financial services products could be sold; and that it would achieve economies of scale through running the estate agencies from one head office.

The company acquired a total of 420 estate agency branches. Shortly afterwards, the property market first began to falter, and then slumped. Property service charges on the estate agency chain became, in the Commercial Union's view, untenable; and plans were made to sell off this part of the business.

In 1994, the estate agency chain was sold on for £1. The purchase price had been £300 million.

While it remains true that there are no certainties in investment, a proper approach to aims, objectives, purpose and risk would have reduced the chances of this level of loss on this venture. Failure to address the medium- to long-term financial returns and requirements meant that effectively the venture was simply based on hopes and expectations.

Box 10.5 *The Bernabeu Football Stadium, Madrid*

The Bernabeu Stadium was first conceived in its present format in 1948. A stadium housing 60,000 people was built. It had the twin purposes of serving as a Spanish national football stadium; it was also to be the permanent home for the Real Madrid Football Club.

The stadium was further developed from 1986 to 1990, to double the capacity to 120,000.

When it was first built, the stadium occupied a position on the northern edge of the City of Madrid. Following extensive urban and commercial development, the stadium is now several miles inside the built-up area.

To be fully successful and effective as a facility, and to maximise the returns on investment, attention has therefore had to be paid to transport, logistics and infrastructure so that 120,000 people can be brought into the stadium at least once a fortnight, and then dispersed from the stadium at the end of the game.

Accordingly, this development led to extensive public transport development, with particular priority placed on the ability of the underground and national railway systems to deliver and disperse this number of people to the facility when required.

This, in turn, led to the generation of an inherent attractiveness of the area, both as a place to live, and also as a place to work. Accordingly, there has been extensive commercial development resulting in a new financial and head office centre (akin to the City of London) directly opposite the stadium to the west. To the east and south of the stadium, property values are among the highest in the city.

The long-term success of the venture can, in summary be ascribed to the following features:

- The integrity of the venture within the existing infrastructure;
- The development of the infrastructure when circumstances changed;
- The long-term commitment envisaged when the stadium was first designed, and the energy and drive of Santiago Bernabeu, the stadium's founder and creator;
- Commitment to continuity of investment in upgrading the facilities and infrastructure when required;
- Attention to the needs and demands of end-users;
- The ability to secure political support and financial backing for the project *in its full context*;
- Attention to other aspects including splendour, prestige and pride;
- Derived investment in the form of continued attention to the outputs of the venture, especially concerning the Real Madrid Football Club.

Clearly where a strategic approach is not present, or not fully evaluated, returns on investment can become less certain to predict. In practice, some of this is compensated for by other factors.

- *'Being the best'*: in whatever terms that is defined; this is very subjective, but nevertheless commands a residual value in investment.
- *Prestige*: again, in whatever terms this is defined. This is largely subjective also, though a certain amount of genuine recognition for achievement can be generated from being 'the first' (in whatever field), 'the biggest', 'the tallest'; and some of this is likely to lead to future work, so long as expertise and returns can be related directly to this form of achievement (see box 10.6).

- *Regeneration*: Especially if driven by government policy, the purpose here is for long-term and derived returns on investment. For example, urban regeneration is undertaken to reduce social problems, improve employment, attract private ventures and increase the propensity to employ, to spend, and therefore to pay taxes. Reductions in policing, welfare and social services are also envisaged.

  The work may either be commissioned directly by government or else indirectly through what is known as 'inward investment', and this is normally supported by grants and incentives (see box 10.7).

- *Maintenance and improvement of existing facilities*, primarily to cope with increased demand for usage, changes in usage, and to meet real and perceived demands for quality of facilities. This form of investment may also be regenerated by public pressure, or real or perceived political pressures to improve something that is deemed to be unacceptable in its present format.

  Less wholesomely, work may be commissioned with one purpose, but with an unstated or hidden agenda (see box 10.8).

- *Individual contributions*, whereby capital investment is proposed as the result of a real or perceived vision or brilliance. Certain individuals take it upon themselves to envisage, propose, outline or design possibilities for the future of cities, towns, areas and regions. Some of these projects come to fruition, others do not. They do at least engage debate and discussion about what could/should/might/must happen as the result of somebody doing something in the given area (see box 10.9).

- *Invention*: Capital investment is here concerned with assessing potential, testing and piloting, bringing into production, and then commercialising the particular invention. The main issue to be aware of here is the entry into pioneering costs. For example, Japanese technological commercialisation has been heavily based on improving existing products, rather than inventing from scratch (the main exception to this is Sony which was founded on inventing and improving magnetic audio tape to the point at which the company's founders were satisfied that it was of a commercial standard, and this process took 16 years).

- *The public good*: This refers to investment in technology, expertise and facilities to improve quality of life. This is particularly applicable to health, education, leisure and social facilities and services. Effective participation in these ventures is normally dependent upon establishing and recouping the project costs in advance and certainly no later than project completion. There are major problems if a substantial part of return on investment accrues only as the result of subsequent usage because it involves arriving at a price-usage formula that is both acceptable to all concerned, and with no potential for corruption by any subsequent dominance–dependency relationship that might arise (see box 10.10).

Box 10.6   *Complexities in capital projects: examples*

- *Assets and liabilities*: In 1999 Blackwell's opened the largest book-shop in the world at Oxford Circus, London. The size of the venture was therefore its main point of attractiveness. So long as the book-shop attracts customers who make purchases, rather than sightseers, in the numbers projected at the inception of the project, it remains an asset. Should the venture fail (in whatever terms ascribed to it by Blackwell's) then the 'asset' becomes a 'liability' – and the company must either find a further use for the site in order to return it to asset status; or it must divest. While this might be dressed up as a 'sale of assets', in practice this is regarded by prospective purchasers as a 'sale of liability', and the price therefore falls;
- *The London Docklands Development Corporation* was established in 1986 to regenerate the Isle of Dogs and Wapping areas of East London following the collapse of the function of London as a major port. Planning regulations were streamlined so that investment could be made attractive. The venture attracted massive capital, and projects were indeed commissioned quickly. The area was trans-formed in seven years from a declining and derelict docklands, into a major second commercial centre for London. It fully exploited the first phase of the development and provided the potential for 150,000 jobs. Attention was not paid to infrastructure, however. Public transport was largely dependent upon the Docklands Light Railway, which was too small to cope with the anticipated volume of traffic. A motorway link was belatedly commissioned (the Dock-lands Expressway, opened in 1993). No mainline railway terminal was commissioned or built. The largest investors, the Reichmann Brothers of Canada, went bankrupt. This was because they were unable to secure long-term enduring perceived benefits that satisfied and real and potential end-users to the extent that they were able to gain returns on their investment;
- *The Bernabeu Stadium and Real Madrid* continue to enjoy the benefits of the long-term commitment, only because they are able, at present, to sustain long-term enduring perceived benefits to the end-users of the facility.

These examples illustrate the tenuous and subjective definitions of assets and liabilities in capital ventures. They also illustrate the potential for, and speed with which, assets can become liabilities, and vice versa.

Box 10.7 *Inward investment in the UK*

As the mass employment industries of the UK collapsed in the 1970s, the policy decision was taken to replace the jobs lost by attracting multinational corporations from overseas to build production and service facilities in specific areas.

This was extensively supported by regional development assistance, start-up grants and public sector investment in road, telecommunications and energy infrastructure; and in relaxing the rules allowing organisations to develop 'greenfield' sites on the edge of industrial areas, rather than being confined to refurbishing existing facilities.

In particular, this has led to the regeneration of the UK car industry, through Nissan, Toyota and Honda; and electronics industry, through Sharp, Sony, Panasonic, Toshiba and Hitachi. While the jobs thus created have not in any way replaced the sheer volume previously lost, the venture has succeeded to an extent in terms of derived investment, because retail distribution and service organisations have been persuaded to develop their activities further in locations where inward investment has taken place.

Inward investment has also been attracted from companies based in Taiwan and South Korea. Inward investment attracted from Europe and North America has been less successful; the most notorious example is Siemens (1995–99). The company was persuaded to locate a European regional office and research facility in Newcastle-upon-Tyne, and to develop a microchip production facility also. Extensive grants were paid. Nevertheless, in September 1998, following the collapse in prices for computer microchips, Siemens took the business decision to pull out of the facility, and to close their operations in the UK, after less then four years' activity.

Box 10.8 *Maintenance and improvement of existing facilities: examples*

M25

The M25 London Orbital motorway project was first proposed in 1970. This was in response to concerns from the London authorities that there was too much traffic passing through the capital, and that therefore this facility would serve to speed up traffic flows overall, and also remove congestion, and therefore pollution, from London.

The project was commenced in 1975, following extensive public opposition in those areas where the motorway was actually to be built. The original facility consisted of a dual carriageway for the full distance of the motorway, with some sections built as triple carriageway.

The motorway has never been able to cope with traffic flows. This is partly because, when it was originally planned, it was assumed that only transit traffic would use it (and that local traffic would not); and partly because the construction of the facility suddenly made it extremely attractive to move goods the length of the country by road (previously, the only way that this could be carried out was by rail).

At the beginning of the twenty-first century, the M25 is being upgraded to provide a basic quadruple carriageway. Rather than objections from environmental protestors and local action groups, the protests are from motoring and transport organisations that the refurbishment and upgrade is not going quickly enough.

Middlesex and University College Hospitals

In 1994 the Middlesex and University College Hospitals were merged into a single University College Hospital Trust. Over the remaining period of the 1990s, the new Trust conducted extensive refurbishment and replacement of existing facilities which were to be paid for by selling off unwanted property that had accrued as the result of the merger.

In fact, no sales of assets were made. In 1998 and 1999 there was a glut of public assets for sale across the whole of the greater London area, and (like many others) the University College Hospital Trust was unable to sell real or perceived property surpluses at anything other than a substantial loss.

In this case, the hidden agenda was in fact fully understood by the finance and property industries and, as the result, two developments have taken place:

- financiers and investors now differentiate between public sector and commercial developments when providing asset valuations;
- the public service approach of paying for future developments through sales of surplus property is no longer an option. Prices simply fall too far when it becomes known that those making the sale are public bodies of any sort.

Box 10.9 *Individual contributions: examples*

It is useful to list briefly some examples, each of which has had varying degrees of success in attracting interest, commitment and investment.

The Thames Corridor

This was first proposed by Michael Heseltine when he was Secretary of State at the Department of Trade and Industry in 1986. The initial proposal was to attract investment to refurbish the entire Kent coast of the River Thames as far east as Chatham. The proposal has resulted in the following.

- The refurbishment of Chatham Dockyards.
- The Bluewater shopping complex.
- The Queen Elizabeth II bridge between Dartford and Purfleet.
- A route for the Channel Tunnel high-speed rail link, taking it through the East End of London and into St Pancras.
- London Town Hall: designed by Norman Foster in 1997 as a unique landmark facility for the south bank of the River Thames near Tower Bridge, and as a fitting monument to the re-creation of the position of Mayor of London as a figure of real political influence. This was driven, in turn, by the commitment of the incoming Labour Government to re-establish the position of Mayor of London, and to make it a high-profile political appointment. It is likely in the medium- to long-term to lead to the demand for, and creation of, politically appointed mayors in other large cities in the UK; and consequently to engage other investment on the back of this.

Internet

Internet investment has been engaged piecemeal and on an *ad hoc* basis over the past decade. Following political interventions in 1999, forms of long-term investment have begun to be engaged by:

- retail and distribution companies, basing their ventures on a potential 4 per cent of the retail and distribution market by the Year 2010;
- the entertainment industry, because the internet can provide alternatives to radio, television, cinema, theatre and compact disks;
- personal services, including travel and estate agency; and also access to personal financial services;

- education: in which it is envisaged that the effectiveness of both school and higher education will depend on access to high-quality information as an integral part of the learning process;
- publishing: by 1997, the internet was already an alternative source of daily newspapers; it is also ripe for exploitation as an alternative source of books, articles, compendia and digests;
- information services companies, and e-business ventures.

The most successful of each of these ventures is certain to be dependent on pioneering work by individuals or small groups working on behalf of the particular organisation commissioning the work. Moreover, it is certain that, in time, internet players will become as high profile as either Cabinet Ministers or as leading architects as they gain for themselves this level of reputation. Many already command very high real and perceived values.

Box 10.10   *The behavioural side of enterprise: examples*

It is useful to draw attention to four examples where the dominance–dependency mixture of the investment relationship may be a real cause for concern.

- *Use of consultants*: Organisations that invest in consultancy services are behaviourally bound by the fees charged by the experts to implement their recommendations and to act upon their advice. It is also true that invariably when problems arise as a result of following the advice, the same consultants become retained to address these issues. Problems arise when a consultant becomes known, believed or perceived to dominate the relationship. It then becomes impossible for shareholders' representatives, other backers, directors or senior managers involved, to do anything about this. The result is that effectively the venture becomes run by the consultants, but without the responsibility for ensuring success or failure.
- *Computer systems*: Problems with computer systems arise when those buying them either do not know precisely what they want, or do not state precisely what they want. This normally arises as the result of a lack of prior consultation with those who are actually to use the systems; and as a result of lack of pinpoint identification as

to what the computer systems themselves are required to do. Accordingly, it is very easy to buy into systems that are overtly attractive and cost effective, but in practice either do not fit operationally or culturally. The problem then becomes one of either replacing the system; or reinventing the culture so that the system can be made to work; or adjusting the system so that it works as well as possible in the circumstances. None of these approaches are fully effective and each adds an on-cost that is never assessed prior to purchase.

- *Health technology*: The problem with health technology lies in its frequency and density of usage in the public sector. Problems with returns on investment in health technology arise when a usage element is built into the costings package. Short-term and expedient budget savings can be demonstrated through mothballing or rationing the usage of particular items of equipment; and returns on investment may never fully be maximised because by the time budget constraints have been relaxed, the next piece of equipment has come along – and may subsequently become subject to the same rationing. This also underlines the point that those who invest in public sector and service activities understand the basis on which the costs and charges involved are to be calculated. In the private sector, return on investment would be maximised by using the equipment as often as possible and this is not always the case in public services.

- *Computers in education*: Those who invest in education technology, or technology for education, may find themselves the subject of contracting supply, cost and price regulation that means that all that can be delivered is something that is not fully up to date, and therefore of little use to the education sector. For example, schools in Kent were still being supplied with pioneering BBC computers seven years after these had been withdrawn from the commercial market. Colleges under the aegis of the Further Education Funding Council were forced into the purchase of administrative and educational packages that were not compatible with each other; in many cases, these were also not compatible across departments or faculties. Also, in the university sector, not until October 1999 did University College London have a fully compatible student recording system that operated across all classes, faculties and divisions. In each of the nineteen colleges of the University of London, education technology has continually failed to be upgraded as the result of budget cuts. Accordingly, the University of London Colleges now require students to have access to their own computers for all undergraduate and diploma courses, and places are offered on the basis that this will be the case.

Start-ups

Some capital investments only come about as the result of start-up or pump-priming activities. These are normally commissioned by macro-bodies such as the UN, NATO, EU and national governments; or else multinational corporations as follows:

- conducting pilot schemes and feasibility studies on particular areas of importance for which they need to attract commercial expertise;
- providing start-up grants and incentives to underwrite initially agreed costs of the venture;
- underwriting potential and insurable risks in the venture. In many cases, this includes insurance against financial and commercial losses;
- engaging consultants, advisers and technical expertise services to work alongside, or in partnership with, the venturers.

The start-up approach to investment only works well when the potential value accrued is demonstrated to the satisfaction of all concerned and in precise measurable terms.

Otherwise the approach is fraught with problems. Promises or clear indications of ventures are delayed or cancelled through political prerogative, and organisational changes of objectives, priorities and direction. The underwriting approach is wasteful and inefficient. Return on investment is often not targeted at all, and rarely precisely targeted. Most of all, such ventures are driven by political expediency (e.g. the need to be seen to be doing something; or to provide a step up the political career ladder for the instigator); or, in cases where multinational corporations become involved, because they are going to receive substantial fees as the result of acting in the interests of the United Nations, NATO or EU. As such, these are of short-term expedient value only; and are cancelled or diluted as soon as the next political imperative comes along.

Options

In capital investment, options come in a variety of forms as follows.

- The option to purchase additional shares in a company or venture. This is offered first to existing investors and is known as a rights issue. Shares are discounted, or rewards for this additional investment are increased, to make the option sufficiently attractive to be bought.
- The option to extend a contracted arrangement provided that it continues to benefit all parties. A secure partnership can then be presented when bidding for further work or seeking further funds.

• The option to develop an existing venture further once it is demonstrated to be successful. For example, Eurotunnel have been awarded the first option to build a further Channel tunnel or to develop the existing facility.
• The option to buy currency and other resources to pay for future investments at present or pre-agreed prices.

Options are attractive to those directly involved in ventures when things are going well because it enables increased levels of return on investment all round. There are two problems which need attention:

• Continuous rights issues eventually cause loss of confidence – shareholders and their representatives begin to wonder where their investment is going, how it is being spent, and whether best use is being made of their funds;
• Dividend levels have to be extended over the new increased volume of shares and, except in the case of extremely profitable ventures, tend to fall in terms of earnings per share.

The equivalent also applies to redevelopment and currency options. Currency options may simply not be sustainable; if the price of one currency has risen or fallen sharply, it may be more cost effective to cancel the deal (incurring whatever charges may be liable) – and re-price the venture in present terms. Redevelopment options may be viewed as an asset, and may be sold on as such, if they are not to be used by the option holder. However, potential buyers will always satisfy themselves that those selling on 'first refusal' redevelopment options are not divesting themselves of something that is no longer worth doing.

PRIVATISATION OF PUBLIC SERVICES AND UTILITIES

The privatisation hypothesis is founded on the premise that public services can be made more efficient and cost effective if they are delivered by commercial bodies working within pre-established government cash payments and spending guidelines; and that nationalised industries are better able to compete if freed from government direction and handed over to those with commercial acumen (Redwood and Letwin, 1983). The public interest is then protected by the creation of regulatory bodies and underpinned by service delivery charters that ensure that value for money continues to be achieved on the part of everyone.

In the UK, over the period since 1984, the following have been wholly or partly privatised:

- research laboratories
- parts of the naval dockyards, together with servicing and defence maintenance contracting
- nationalised railway, road transport and airline services
- telecommunications
- the energy sector
- parts of social services
- parts of education services (especially higher education)
- information services
- airports and air traffic control.

In addition, many parts of other public activities have been part-privatised or else attract charges. This especially applies to: parts of the health service; the prison service; waste disposal; highways maintenance and management; town and country planning; infrastructure development; and information services and technology.

Each of these areas is supported by a regulatory body, a consumer council, and an ombudsman. These are established to make reports to Parliament and central government authorities under whose aegis each sits; and also to address concerns and complaints brought to them by members of the public. These regulators also have roles in establishing quality standards, assuring that these are maintained and delivered, and establishing the price and charge levels. They also impose penalty clauses on those that fail to deliver adequate services (see box 10.11).

Box 10.11   *The privatisation of public services and utilities*

The stated view of privatising public services was to improve them on the basis that, if they were put out to commercial pressures, then quality would be driven up, and costs down. In practice, with two exceptions – British Telecommunications and British Airways – what happened was very different.

The original Letwin-Redwood thesis was aimed at driving down costs in bureaucracies, rather than hiving off the essential UK industries and infrastructure. However, the government bureaucracies have never been put out to tender, nor have they been reduced in size or increased in efficiency. The Letwin-Redwood thesis foresaw the central government bureaucracy of 20,000; at the beginning of the twenty-first century it is 660,000, almost exactly the same as in 1982 when *Privatising the World* was published.

Other problems have become apparent.

- Those that sought long-term investment in privatisation found themselves subsequently being taken over or bought out by initiatives from other organisations that were too large or powerful to be resisted.
- Regulatory bodies have found it impossible to control or raise standards for either those seeking long-term investment in privatisation ventures, or for the customer and client groups served.
- With the exception of telecommunications and air travel, all ventures have resulted in a poorer quality of product and service, delivered at lesser cost effectiveness.
- There have been short- to medium-term share 'churning' advantages (i.e. buying shares at early prices and selling them on after a period of 2–5 years) but no genuine venture opportunities otherwise.
- Many smaller ventures, especially those in health, social and prison services, have found themselves open to charges of profiteering. The same accusation has also been levelled at those who have acquired the privatised franchises (especially road and rail services).

Investment opportunities in privatisation continue to exist. However, they are partial and need to be seen as such. Financial consultants and other advisers to government have been sure to collect their fees in advance of any long-term outcome of the venture. Enterprise restructuring consultants continue to be able to sell their expertise overseas, though this is normally tied into government and EU aid packages (see box 10.12).

Others invest in privatised utilities – gas, electricity, water and telecommunications – as part of a portfolio of activities. While these products and services are subject to price regulation there remains, nevertheless, the ability to sell basic social requirements of energy, water, transport and telecommunications over the long term to a captive market, thus ensuring a basic level of guaranteed income against what captive markets are able (rather than willing) to pay. As such, share prices are likely to remain high enough to reflect their value that they are as safe a long-term investment as anything (see box 10.13).

Box 10.12   *Polish State Railways*

Poland is set to join the European Union in the Year 2001; or as soon as possible thereafter. As a condition of this, the EU has required substantial increases in standards of living, and quality of working and social life. One of the core planks of this has been the insistence on the privatisation of nationalised industries and services.

Accordingly, the Polish state railway is to be privatised on the same basis as that which took place in the United Kingdom. Each route on the railways is to be opened up to tender; and franchises of between 7 and 30 years are to be sold. Existing EU railway transport venture and financial interest is to be allowed. The only condition is that there must be a local partner drawn from the ranks of companies registered in Poland. The railway lines, station facilities, signalling and railway maintenance are to be established in a company akin to Railtrack plc, the UK provider.

This, it is perceived, is to draw in hard currency injections, that will, in turn, lead to further development in the country, and, in the medium to long term, the establishment of an industrial and commercial base well within the standards established across the rest of the European Union.

Box 10.13   *Moral pricing*

Moral pricing is the phrase that is applied to charges made on the essentials of life, for which an economic rent clearly exists.

The moral price is arrived at through a nebulous combination of:

- the price that ought to be charged;
- the price that people ought to be prepared to pay;
- a fair return on investment;
- social unacceptability of charging full commercial fees for the absolute necessities of life.

A key function of privatisation regulators is to ensure that prices are kept within these tenuous and subjective boundaries. Problems arise either when companies use their position of dominance to force charges up; or when government tries to cap charges for political and social reasons. Again, the result is that the product or service is delivered to lower quality standards, and to lesser cost advantages, than when under previous government control; or when commercial prices are put on real and perceived public necessities.

OTHER FACTORS AND ISSUES

Private Finance Initiative

Private Finance Initiative (PFI) investments are likely to continue to prove attractive, so long as:

(1) the scale of the venture is fully evaluated, rather than being limited to concentration on the short-term perceived advantages;
(2) the contract rules transcend any political changes that may take place over the period of the project. This is especially important in civil and construction engineering projects, which have lease periods of between 9 and 50 years at present.

Also for those who invest in these ventures, it is essential that agreements are reached at the inception about what is to happen to the project, product or service at the end of the lease or contracted period (see box 10.14).

Box 10.14   *The British Embassy, Berlin*

In 1996 the UK government invited bids to build, own and operate the proposed new embassy building in Berlin. The site chosen was on the Unter den Linden, in the centre of the city; it was being commissioned as part of the rebuilding of what used to be East Berlin. Near the new Reichstag building, it occupies a prime site, both from a public and commercial point of view.

It was proposed that, when completed, the embassy would be leased back to the UK government for a period of 37 years at a rental set initially at £19 million per annum, linked to the retail prices index. No British contractor could be found to bid for the work. In the end a shortlist was drawn up – one of the contractors was French, one German, and one Japanese.

The contract was awarded to Shimizu, the Japanese building and civil engineering multinational. This was the only company that could be persuaded to take a positive view of the need to commit to the 37-year lease. Of overriding value to Shimizu, however, was the option whether to re-negotiate the lease at the end of the period; or to offer it as a commercial facility to the private sector on the assumption that Berlin would still, in 37 years time, be the most important city in the European Union.

PFI service contracts are also attractive to the investor, because they are based on pre-agreed and guaranteed levels of income. While these may not necessarily be high, they are more or less certain as steady-state business because they are being paid by the government; there is therefore no (or very little) prospect of inability to keep up payments or bankruptcy. They are additionally attractive at present because the political view is that, in the short to medium term, it reduces capital charges on the public purse.

Social Investment

At present there is a generally favourable attitude towards the principle of social investment; and some organisations have become to take real initiatives in this area. For example, Royal and Sun Alliance has lent its name to a nation-wide initiative to encourage businesses to support anti-drugs projects, and to sponsor particular inner-city projects and ventures; and NatWest, FI Group and Morgan Stanley have all underwritten voluntary organisations concerned with tackling the problems of home-lessness.

Superficially attractive, the key problem lies in managing the driving financial forces in these circumstances. Corporate investors, especially, still require to see the contribution that such ventures are going to make to the overall effectiveness of their investment before they are prepared to commit to involvement in long-term socially oriented ventures. It is therefore essential to be clear at the outset where the boundaries of the relationship are to lie, and also to address the proposed length of involvement.

Other organisations are beginning to require staff to be involved in community ventures and projects as part of their continuing obligations to the organisation, off-the-job training, or as a fully integrated term and condition of employment (the first organisation to do this was Body Shop, which in 1982 required all its employees to engage in one day's community service per month).

The other key factor that has to be addressed is the measurement of returns on this form of investment. Clearly finance is not a full answer; however, no model exists for the measurement of medium- to long-term derived financial gains that accrue as the result of this form of engagement – and this applies both to investors, and to society at large (see box 10.15).

Lease or Buy

Consider the example shown in Figure 10.1. As a simple, financial calculation, it is overtly straightforward to decide to buy the equipment. However, the following points need to be taken into account.

- When leasing, it is normal to take into account servicing and maintenance arrangements; and many leasing arrangements now also allow for replacements, improvements and upgrades.
- The problem is further complicated if the decision to buy includes a residual value at the end of the projected lifespan. For example, if this piece of equipment had a residual value of £20,000, then overtly the decision to buy is reinforced. However, at the end of the period it may not be possible actually to get £20,000 for the piece of equipment. In particular, if it becomes known that capital equipment is being sold off because it is no longer required, the price always falls. Maintenance charges would also have to be borne as a result of the decision to buy.
- The decision to lease may tie the investor into prescribed and preordained maintenance periods, which may be at variance with the production and output requirements; the extent to which this can be varied also needs consideration.
- If there are any problems with the leased machinery, it is normal to include replacement as part of the contracted arrangement.
- While the lease requires double the simple payment, this is not required in advance of production, and so the lease payments can be tied in with productivity, output and income derived, thus reducing cash-flow problems in the short to medium term.
- Problems with the lease would arise if the equipment ceased to have value after a period of, say, two or three years; in this case, problems would arise if the leasing company insisted that the lease was paid up in full.

It is therefore clearly a complex decision; and to maximise its effect, a much broader perspective has to be taken than a simple financial calculation. The decision to buy, all things being equal, is likely to be taken on the basis that the company can afford it; the company can afford, if not tolerate, a full write-off; the product or information output is of medium- to long-term enduring value; this would be reinforced if it was to a familiar, stable or expanding market.

A small engineering company needs a new electronic production line. Its estimated useful life is five years. The company may either buy the equipment for £100,000 or lease it for £40,000 per annum.

Clearly for each option, the total costs are:

- Leasing: 5 × £40,000 = £200,000.
- Buying: £100,000 + the cost of any finance or overdraft interest charges. While it may be necessary to pay for the equipment in full at the point of purchase, this charge may nevertheless be offset by making an accounting allowance over the five years or over any other period that the accountant sees fit.

Figure 10.1 *To lease or buy: example*

Box 10.15   *Social investment*

The boundaries within which the measurement of social investment takes place are as follows.

Government Priorities

At the beginning of the twenty-first century, government priorities are ordered and devised by focus groups, policy studies institutes and other public policy experts. In most cases, the remit is to produce a report or set of proposals which it is then hoped, expected or anticipated will be carried forward by anyone whose interest is engaged as a result. Because of the vagueness and indetermination surrounding what happens to such proposals once they are published, potential social investors normally require any venture to be fully underwritten and guaranteed by the particular arm of government before a commitment to purpose can be assured.

Expertise

At the beginning of the twenty-first century, those with knowledge and expertise in areas of social concern invariably have very little influence. Above all, their lobbying power to persuade institutions to back ventures with long-term funding is extremely limited. The particular constraint is therefore best managed through seeking to ensure annual donations from organisations; and this is clearly at risk of reduction or cancellation should there be a change in ownership or status of the donating organisations.

Results

As stated above, the measurement of this form of investment is extremely difficult to achieve. It is also true that the potential divergence and conflict between results measured in social, financial and corporate reputation terms, has to be addressed and reconciled.

Clearly then, these are very broad boundaries within which such ventures are contemplated. It is also clear that those with responsibility for investment activities are likely to head towards those areas in which outcomes can be predicted with a greater degree of certainty.

The decision would be informed by relatively high payments in return for lack of worries; a more volatile product service or information output; more volatile or less certain markets; the choice not to commit resources in advance.

The decision may also be coloured one way or the other by the prevailing views of dominant or powerful interests. For example, a finance company may insist that the equipment is leased, and that the lease is arranged through them, so that they gain a residual benefit in the form of guaranteed interest payments. Or the equipment manufacturer may insist that the technology is leased first of all so that it can assess the performance without taking the risk that, if the equipment was bought and then failed in some way, it would have no control over any adverse publicity or effects on reputation.

The lease or buy decision is of especial importance when considering investment in information technology. This is clearly because the capability and capacity of this technology is growing in both quality and quantity, while the price is falling steadily.

It is also essential that such technology is not bought in purely on grounds of prestige. Superficially attractive though it may be to have access to the very latest equipment available today, the basic questions:

- is it appropriate for us?
- what can it do for us?
- how long will it last?
- how are we going to measure returns on this investment?

still have to be asked; and this has to be reinforced by ensuring that staff, and anyone else required to use it, or dependent on its outputs, are familiar and comfortable with it.

CONCLUSIONS

The purpose of this chapter has been to bring the various threads of the book together, and to either demonstrate or reflect these in the main situations in which investments and ventures take place.

From this, it can be seen that:

- No clear or universal set of criteria exist for the measurement of investment; this is a matter for consideration by those seeking to enter into particular ventures; each venture is unique, and therefore requires its own individually agreed set of criteria.

• Overtly similar ventures may produce very different results; it is therefore necessary to identify criteria specific to each venture on which the basis of effective investment can be drawn up.

Measurement

At the beginning of the twenty-first century maximised short- to medium-term shareholder value remains the driving force. This remains true, despite the fact that every other drive is towards long-term sustainability and viability, whether in personal finance or capital project returns. It is compounded also by the pressures of the annual and interim reporting cycles; and the short-term profits share and interest performances that contribute positively or negatively to each.

Anyone wishing to depart from this line has therefore to be capable of presenting the ways in which they calculate the success or otherwise of a venture; and to get this accepted by those with both knowledge and influence. The problem is compounded further still because this forces investors and venturers:

(a)   to establish their own precise criteria in areas often unfamiliar to themselves;
(b)   to look away from the familiar (if imperfect) annual cycles, profit or mark-up margins, and short-term share values, and into something which, while it may be a much better way of measuring performance, is nevertheless unknown and unfamiliar (and therefore untried and untested) – see box 10.16.

Box 10.16   *The attractions of EVA*

The investment world is as prone as any other to fashion, and the current craze gripping analysts and fund managers is a whole set of allegedly new measures of what constitutes value.

Words like 'shareholder value', 'enterprise value' and 'economic value added' may cause the average investor's eyes to glaze over, but they are being used increasingly to justify job cuts, share buy-backs, de-mergers and selling companies.

• *Shareholder value*: Many experts trace the origins of the new crop of value measures to the work of two Nobel prize-winning economists,

Franco Modigliani and Merton Miller, who came up with a new theory of how to measure the cost of equity. This involves balancing share values with other asset values, both tangible and intangible, to assess the effectiveness of capital usage.

- *Economic value added*: The current fashionable valuation theory is EVA – economic value added. EVA is calculated by taking the profits for a year and deducting from them a charge for the cost of capital. A company has to earn more than it pays for the money it uses in its business, otherwise it cannot make profits. The difference is that EVA attempts to look at it from the investor's point of view.
- *Economic profits*: The first task of EVA is to level the playing field by adjusting a company's profits to make them comparable with other firms. This may involve capitalising interests, research and development costs, or, in asset-based businesses, changing the depreciation charge.
- *Cost of capital*: Deducted from the economic profit is the company's cost of capital. The EVA cost of capital involves the addition of three components – risk-free return; market risk premium; and a company's risk premium. The result is an interest rate that can be applied to the capital used in the company tied up in equipment, stocks, cash and other assets, to come up with the cost of capital.
- *Enterprise value*: Enterprise value is based on earnings before interest, tax and depreciation that cuts out three charges prone to accounts creativity. Because the debt charge is being excluded on one side of the equation, it must be added back on the other, so that a company's enterprise value is measured by its stock market value plus borrowings.

Clearly, the problem with this approach is that it seeks to replace the simplistic and familiar with the complex and unfamiliar. From a behavioural point of view, it is therefore certain to be rejected by those who are not experts in the field. Any attempt to reform the measurement of investment and to generate a greater all-round understanding of what ventures are supposed to, and required to, produce must take an alternative route. It must also be capable of presentation in such a way as to gain a wider, more familiar and more universal acceptance over present approaches. Finally, as the source makes clear, the approach is 'fashionable' and therefore transient and subjective.

Source: Magnus Grimmond, 'Getting the Measure of a New Fashion in Assessing Values', *Evening Standard*, 13 September 1999.

A Note on the DotCom Revolution

Investment in Internet companies is driven by the real and perceived opportunity to take advantage of the huge volume of information available, on the one hand, and the equally vast potential access afforded by computer and telecommunications technology, on the other. Consequently, Internet companies have been able to attract both corporate and individual investors to make substantial investments. For example, Lastminute.com, an online travel and airline ticket sales company, was able, in March 2000, to attract investment of £850,000 million at a time when its annual turnover was £1.6 million, with an annual operating loss of £24 million.

Anyone seeking a business-related return on investment is overtly committed to a period of anything up to ten years before they get their money back. There is a widely held perception that, in reality, the time scale is certain to be shorter than this; and that returns are certain to increase as using the Internet becomes more familiar to customers and easier to use for everyone. However, there is at present no substantial evidence defining the speed at which those people with Internet access are going to turn their general interest into commercial consumption – to translate ability to use into willingness to use. Neither have companies or investors given any indication that they have thought seriously about customer volumes, characteristics, or aspirations; nor have measures of success or value been thought of in terms of income per customer, benefits available, and product and service values.

From the investor's point of view, the stock market is sanguine. In March 2000, Anthony Impey, General Manager of Touchbase Plc, stated 'Investment in Internet opportunities and the DotCom revolution represents 0.5% of total investment volumes only. Of the first wave of companies floated on the stock exchange, 97% are expected not to exist in their present form in five years' time. Many will fail; others will merger; others still will be taken over. Of those that do still exist at the end of the period, a similar shakeout is expected over the following five years.'

He also went on to put forward the view that when – not if – the fall in values came around, it would be the entrepreneurs themselves and small private investors, not big institutions, who would lose their investment.

Consequently, investment in the DotCom revolution is seen in many quarters as little more than speculation, and certainly value measurement and establishing criteria for success have to be seen in this context. Another view is that there are parallels between the Internet explosion and the first UK industrial revolution of 1750–1850. Entrepreneurs, technologists, inventors and others with creative talents are backing themselves and seeking financial investments to turn invention and inspiration into long-term sustainable commercial viability, just as engineering, textile and transport entrepreneurs did 250 years ago. At that time also, return on investment was

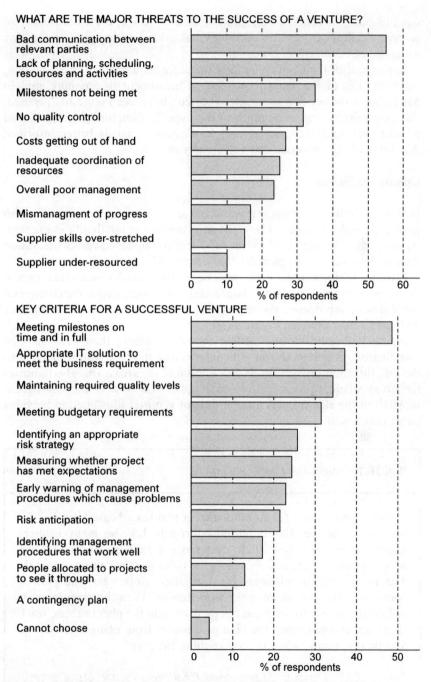

WHAT ARE THE MAJOR THREATS TO THE SUCCESS OF A VENTURE?

KEY CRITERIA FOR A SUCCESSFUL VENTURE

Source: Bull Information Systems, *Information Week*, 21 October 1998.

Figure 10.2 *Key criteria for venture success*

not capable of prediction or guarantee, and there was a huge incidence of company failure, collapse, bankruptcy, takeover and merger – and a tiny incidence of fulfilment of potential.

Investment in DotCom companies therefore requires the same attention, and adoption of the same principles, as investment in anything else. In particular, if the venture approach indicated above (see Figure 10.2) is used, this may help to strip away much of the hype, fashion and glamour that at present surrounds the sector, and lead towards much better informed decision-making processes and value analyses.

Criteria for Success

Inadequate criteria for the measurement of investment performance also arise as a result of a general lack of understanding or familiarity in the area. Again, therefore, there is a tendency to stick to simplistic approaches, rather than addressing the complexities that are actually involved.

Effective performance criteria must be related to each of the areas covered in previous pages – strategy, culture and behaviour, decision-making and commitment to purpose, risk, units of measurement, and the effectiveness of investment relations (see Figure 10.2).

Figure 10.2 indicates one method by which each of these areas may be investigated, as well as showing the importance to those who responded to the Bull Information Systems Survey of each of the areas. This also indicates the areas where the least attention is paid and reflects the consequent shortfall in the effectiveness and outputs of ventures illustrated in previous pages (see box 10.17).

Box 10.17   *Bulldozers move mountains*

'Analysis may show for instance that a planner's beautiful plans die because he or she does not follow through. Like so many brilliant people, he or she believes that ideas move mountains. But bulldozers move mountains; ideas show where the bulldozers have to go to work. The most brilliant planners far too often stop when the plan is completed. But that is when the work begins. Then the planner needs to find the people to carry out the plan, explain the plan to them, teach them, adapt and change the plan as it moves from planning to doing, and finally, decide when to stop pushing the plan'.

Source: P. F. Drucker, *Management Challenges for the 21st Century*, HarperCollins, 1999.

Both of these approaches reinforce the point that it is attention to factors other than narrow or linear financial projections that make the difference between success and failure in investment ventures. Ventures that fail are those that concentrate on financial and output projections rather than considering the uncertainties and vagaries of each of those factors that contribute to the financial and output projections (see box 10.18).

Box 10.18 *The management of ventures and projects*

'A large proportion of project management work of any significant size is not technical. However, many managers assume it's just common sense and see no need for specific training so the new project manager often puts the emphasis in the wrong place. Project management is common sense, but structured common sense.

The main reasons for loss of control on most ventures are aggressive timescales, moving goalposts, fast moving technology, reduced budgets, resource limitations and staff turnover – all of which most professionals have not normally been trained for. Also, interpersonal skills are vital for successful project and venture management and need to be developed through training. It is usually the financial and management considerations that an untrained professional will find most difficult.'

Source: Andrew Harrison (1998) quoted in Janine Milne,
'Management: Master Plans Pay Off', *Information Week*,
21 October 1998.

Most importantly, the problem lies in managing the diverse and conflicting interests, and reconciling the different outputs required from particular ventures. It is essential that, for anything to be successful, the conditions are created in which this can take place in advance of projects and ventures being commissioned. It is also essential to jump this hurdle as a prerequisite fully to informing the chances of successful ventures in investment. It is finally certain that those who do appraise ventures and investments from the broadest perspective are more certain to secure long-term and enduring success and the confidence that goes with this than those who do not.

Select Bibliography

Ansoff, H. I. (1985) *Business Strategy*, Penguin.

Buchholz, R. (1982) *Business Environment and Public Policy*, Prentice Hall International.

Butcher, H. (1999) *Information for Management and Decision-Making*, AsLib.

Cartwright, R. (1994) *In Charge of Finance*, Blackwell.

Cartwright, R. (1997) *In Charge: Managing Yourself*, Blackwell.

Cartwright, R. and Baird, C. (1999) *The Growth and Development of the Cruise Industry*, Butterworth Heinemann.

Christensen, C. R. (1990) *Business Policy*, Irwin.

Dixon, R. (1994) *Investment Appraisal: A Guide for Managers*, Kogan Page.

Drucker, P. F. (1999) *Management Challenges for the 21st Century*, HarperCollins.

Ellis, J. and Williams, B. (1990) *Corporate Strategy and Financial Analysis*, F.T. Pitman.

Griseri, P. (1997) *Managing Values*, Macmillan.

Handy, C. B. (1990) *Understanding Organisations*, Penguin.

Handy, C. B. (1994) *The Future of Work*, Penguin.

Heller, R. (1980) *The Naked Manager*, Coronet.

Layard, R. (1982) *Cost Benefit Analysis*, Penguin.

Letwin, O. and Redwood, J. (1982) *Privatising the World*, Policy Studies Institute.

Luthans, F. (1989) *Organisational Behaviour*, McGraw-Hill.

O'Neil, J. J. (1989) *Management of Industrial and Construction Projects*, Heinemann.

Peters, T. and Waterman R. H. (1980) *In Search of Excellence*, Harper & Row.

Pettinger, R. (1997) *Introduction to Management*, Macmillan.

Pettinger, R. and Frith, R. (1996) *Measuring Business and Managerial Performance*, F.T. Pitman.

Porter, M. E. (1982) *Competitive Strategy*, Macmillan.

Porter, M. E. (1986) *Competitive Advantage*, Macmillan.

Potter, D. C. (1980) *Decisions, Organisations and Society*, Penguin.

Semler, R. (1992) *Maverick*, Free Press.

Sternberg, E. (1994) *Just Business*, Warner.

Walker, K. (1998) *Creating New Clients*, Cassell.

Wright, M. G. (1980) *Financial Management*, McGraw-Hill.

Index

221